California Natural History Guides: 9

INTRODUCTION TO

SEASHORE LIFE

OF THE

SAN FRANCISCO BAY REGION

AND THE

COAST OF NORTHERN CALIFORNIA

BY

JOEL W. HEDGPETH

ILLUSTRATED BY THE AUTHOR AND LYNN RUDY

CALIFORNIA NATURAL HISTORY GUIDES

Arthur C. Smith, General Editor

UNIVERSITY OF CALIFORNIA PRESS
BERKELEY AND LOS ANGELES, CALIFORNIA
UNIVERSITY OF CALIFORNIA PRESS, LTD.
LONDON, ENGLAND

LIBRARY OF CONGRESS CATALOG CARD NUMBER: 62-17534
PRINTED IN THE UNITED STATES OF AMERICA
SIXTH PRINTING, 1975
ISBN: 0-520-02992-5 (CLOTHBOUND)
0-520-00544-9 (PAPERBOUND)

CONTENTS

NOTE ON ILLUSTRATIONS.

The drawings of crabs and seashells are by Lynn Rudy. In Plate 1, the photograph of Pescadero is by the author; all others are by Robert D. Mir. In Plate 2, the photograph of *Anthopleura xanthogrammica* is by Jerry Rudy; that of *Hermissenda crassicornis* is by Robert D. Mir; all others are by Tay Sloan. In Plate 3, the photographs of *Anisodoris nobilis* and of *Triopha maculata* are by Robert D. Mir; that of pycnogonids and caprellid is by Woody Williams; the painting of *Pachygrapsus crassipes* is by Alberté Spratt; the photograph of sea lions and sea elephants is by the author. Plate 4 is from a painting by Norman Mayer. Plates 5-8 are by the author. Cover photograph by Tay Sloan.

THE ENVIRONMENT OF THE SHORE

The seashore is one of the most interesting of all natural regions to both casual visitor and professional naturalist. This is not only because of the great variety and abundance of creatures that live in the sea, and the difference of this life from what we know on land, but also because of the changes that may occur with each change of tide. Always there is something just a little different along the beach with each change of the tide, and few people walk there without the hope that something strange and wonderful has been freshly cast up by the sea.

In the Bay region we are fortunate in having a wide variety of shore habitats, many of them rich in seashore life, attracting students from all parts of the world to come and study some aspect or another of this varied life. Two local centers for such study are Hopkins Marine Station, maintained by Stanford University at Pacific Grove, and Pacific Marine Station of the University of the Pacific, at Dillon Beach. As this is being written, the University of California has announced plans for a third marine laboratory in the region, at Bodega Head.

Most of the northern California coast is sheer and rocky and exposed to the full force of the waves. Here and there, behind offshore stacks and in small coves, there are good localities to observe marine life. One of the best on the Sonoma County coast is Shell Beach, just below the mouth of the Russian River; it is especially fine for seaweeds, sea urchins, and seastars. As this is a State Park, collecting of marine life is theoretically forbidden. The finest rocky headland of the Sonoma Coast is Bodega Head, with some beautiful tidepools at Horseshoe Cove. Behind Bodega Head are excellent sand and mud flats, and the jetties at Bodega Harbor provide much of interest. Bold, sheer headlands like Point Reyes are not the best place to see marine life

[5]

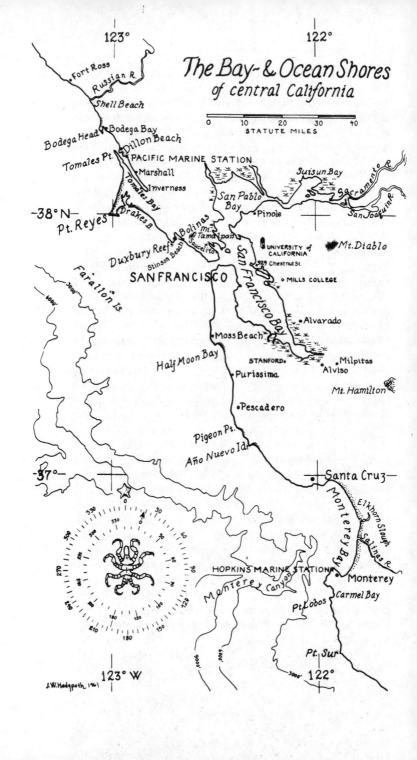

because the abrupt, vertical surfaces and the heavy wave action make exploration dangerous. Marin County provides several fine, accessible localities around Dillon Beach, along the shores of Tomales Bay, and on the rocky ocean coast of Tomales Point. Also in Marin County, near Bolinas, is Duxbury Reef, a formation of soft shale, especially fine for boring clams and animals nestling within old borings. Traveling south, the next site of particular biological interest is Moss Beach in San Mateo County. This area of low reefs, once much richer than in recent years, is visited by people collecting the edible sea urchins and turban shells, and by battalions of students on field trips. Between Moss Beach and Pacific Grove are several good localities, restricted in variety of habitat, such as Pigeon Point and Año Nuevo Island. The coarse granite headlands of Pacific Grove and Carmel provide many sheltered coves and tidepools that are world-famous collecting spots. To the south, the coast is so sheer and inaccessible that few good collecting grounds are to be found until one nears San Luis Obispo. Between these various fine rocky sites are four sand beaches: Salmon Creek Beach in Sonoma County, 14-Mile Beach in Marin, Half Moon Bay in San Mateo County, and Sunset Beach in Santa Cruz and Monterey counties. Below the Golden Gate there is but one good sheltered mud flat area, Elkhorn Slough.

Although the shore of San Francisco Bay (including San Pablo Bay) is more than 150 miles long, most of it consists of city waterfronts, salt marshes, sloughs, and mud flats. There are rocky shores around San Rafael, Tiburon, and Richmond in the north, and at Coyote Point near San Mateo in the south part of the bay. Salt marshes have a peculiar charm, and while the fauna of the rocky bay shores is limited, both regions of the bay shores—as all regions—are interesting to the naturalist. Wherever there are docks in water reasonably free from substances inimical to life, a luxuriant growth of animals and plants develops on the piling, and many of the organisms found on piling are rare elsewhere.

Many of our well-known localities are suffering from too much visitation by bait gatherers, epicures, and student groups. While we hope this book will stimulate interest in the seashore, we hope also that such interest will be an understanding one, an interest that prefers to leave things where they are and to observe the plants and animals of the seashore in nature, rather than to carry them off in buckets. Many people take such things as seastars, urchins, crabs, and anemones home, only to find them dead on arrival, or to have their aquarium turn foul in a few days. Marine aquaria must be refrigerated to temperatures near that of the sea, and few homes have such aquarium equipment. It is better to leave things where they are, both for yourself and for other people. With the increasing interest in science in our schools has come an almost overwhelming pressure of school groups, and it is common now for several hundred students, representing schools from many parts of northern California, to descend on the beaches at favorable low tides. For the sake of others who must come the next day or the fortnight after, we suggest that teachers impress upon their charges the necessity for returning rocks to their places, and that they emphasize the advantages of being able to study seashore life as it is, alive in nature. Many people in the middle of this continent never have this opportunity, and it should not be accepted lightly, nor sacrificed in favor of a bucket of moribund, soggy loot. If collecting is considered necessary, it should be closely supervised and carried out with some purpose in mind. If you must collect, do not use glass containers, for broken glass cannot be seen in sea water and the next person may get badly cut.

TEMPERATURE

Although the habitats range from sheer cliffs and reefs richly covered with life to apparently barren sandy

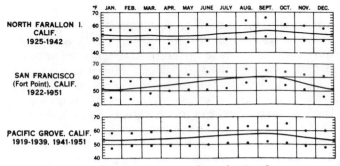

Average surface temperatures along the Pacific coast
(From U. S. C. & G. S.)

beaches, the most influential factor controlling distribution of marine life along the ocean shore is temperature, and on this coast the range of temperature throughout the year is relatively narrow. Near Point Reyes and the Farallons the monthly averages range from 52.4° during April to 56.3° in September, while at Pacific Grove the lowest monthly average is 53° in January, and the high again is in September, at 57.3°. Our ocean waters near shore, then, are cold, and the temperatures are fairly even (of course, there are days when the ocean will be much colder or warmer than these average figures), although from year to year there are fluctuations of several degrees from these averages. Still, the water is cold, and we consider this a "cold temperate" region; indeed, northern California has some of the coldest sea temperatures, for its latitude, on the globe. In bays and sheltered regions temperatures are often much higher.

The reasons for this cold water along our ocean coast are somewhat complex. These cold temperatures are associated with the process known as upwelling, the movement toward the surface of cold subsurface water from a few score or hundred feet below. This is induced by the action of the prevailing wind from the northwest, which pushes the surface water away from the land. The water does not move directly before the wind, but angles off to the right of the direction of the wind, so the effect of wind from the northwest along a coast running approximately in the same direction is to push the surface water away from shore. Thus, water upwells from lower levels to take the place of this wind-driven water. This is not going on all the time, of course, and there are periods when surface waters move up from the south. During some years this whole system may be upset and then we have warmer temperatures, perhaps a few degrees higher on the average. But life in a region like this is adjusted to a narrow range of temperatures, and slight changes can influence distribution to such an extent that animals common at Pacific Grove may turn up at Dillon Beach, and sharks appear on the scene to upset swimmers. The causes of these fluctuations must be sought in an analysis of the entire wind and current system of the Pacific Ocean, and we do not yet understand this system very well.

When this wind system weakens, as it did in 1957, the intensity of upwelling decreases and warm water from the south moves farther to the north. Fishes, such as the sardine, whose eggs hatch best at certain temperatures, may be slowed down in development several days by a drop of only one or two degrees, and this pro-

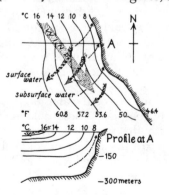

How upwelling occurs

longed development lengthens their exposure to all the dangers of being eaten or hatching abnormally. Thus, slight changes in temperature can affect survival ten-fold, adversely or favorably, depending on the organism concerned. The period of colder water along the California coast from 1947 to 1956 probably had as much, if not more, to do with the decline of the sardine fishery as did the intensive fishing that kept the canneries of Monterey going in their halcyon days. Indeed, some marine biologists are of the opinion that man's influence on the populations of the open sea is still insignificant, although it has been abundantly demonstrated that fishing does have a direct influence on bottom feeding fishes such as flounders, cod, and halibut.

WAVES

The action of tides and waves is often confused: a "tidal wave" has nothing to do with the tide but is induced by earthquake activity on the floor of the ocean. The true tidal wave is the rise and fall of the tide—a

Eddy formed as crest approaches

Eddy rises as crest passes

Eddy disperses as trough passes

Sorting action of a wave as it moves shoreward (to the right), lifting fine material that is dispersed seaward as the trough breaks up the eddy

[11]

long wave that usually has two rises and falls a day in this part of the coast. Most of the waves we see are induced by the wind, and since we have wind at least 60% of the time in this region, days of flat calm are rare. A wave is essentially an up and down movement of water, and most of the actual movement of objects we associate with wave action is accomplished at the shore as the waves break or tip forward. A circular motion of water is set up, with most of the carrying force directed shoreward, with the result that larger objects from pebbles to whales are moved up the beach and finer material is carried back with the receding water. This action also sets up wave-like bars and finer ripples in the sand bottom. These structures are moved shoreward, acting somewhat as movable riffle bars, to carry the larger sand grains and pebbles forward; thus, where wave action is usually strong, the beach sand is coarser. Where the sea is very rough, we have beaches of pebbles and sometimes of cobbles. Most of the receding water from wave action is at the surface, not at the bottom as "undertow," and it is possible to see from the air the streamers of surface water returning to the sea at various places along the shore. "Undertow" as such is a popular misconception, but frightened swimmers cannot distinguish between the upsetting turbulence of waves and some mysterious force which seems to be dragging them to sea by "towing them under." To be sure, there is dangerous turbulence at times of very strong wave action (when most people stay out of the water anyhow), and it seems fitting to conclude this discussion with the following succinct paragraph from Russell and Macmillan's *Waves and Tides*:

Granted that on occasion there is an undertow, and this is particularly likely when steep waves and an on-shore wind are pushing the surface water towards the shore, the question at issue is whether a swimmer can be taken out to sea by it. The answer is no. A swimmer is necessarily affected more by the surface water than the bottom water, and consequently, when there is an undertow, he is likely to be carried towards the shore. If he sinks, he may be carried seawards; but if he sinks he has passed from the category of swimmers.

As for the "tidal wave" which oceanographers call "tsunami," this is a fast moving wave, traveling several hundred miles an hour from the site of a major submarine earthquake. In the North Pacific these waves may start from Japan or the Aleutian Islands and travel across the ocean in a few hours. The damage and loss of life caused by these waves depend upon local geography as much as on the force of the wave, and certain parts of the Hawaiian Islands are especially vulnerable. Tsunamis have not been seriously damaging on the California coast, but the Chilean earthquakes during the spring of 1960 set in motion a tsunami that caused damage to boats and docks as far north as Crescent City.

As waves near the shore, two things happen. It is the tendency of waves to become parallel to the shore, so that their direction ("orthogonal") is at right angles ("normal") to the shore. As a result, when waves reach a headland they tend to converge against both sides of it, causing the heavy breaking that is so conspicuous on

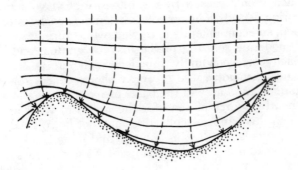

Wave refraction on the coast

days of rough seas. Conversely, waves tend to flatten out and level off between headlands.

The other event is the conversion of a wave to surf, which is caused by shortening the wave length as the bottom shoals, so that the actual speed of the wave is increased until the forward motion at the top of the wave is greater than at the bottom, and the wave breaks to become surf. The height of a plunging breaker, with a well-defined hollow front, is about the same as the depth of the water. Most of such large, plunging breakers are formed by storm waves which may be generated thousands of miles from the coast. The waves which reach the shore are usually a mixture of several sets of waves from different storms or winds, and as a result there is often a mixture of various wave heights as the waves of one sequence dampen or augment the waves of another. This sequence varies from day to day, so it is not correct to say that every "seventh" or "ninth" wave" is the highest.

On a sandy beach the action results in movement of sand along the beach; the direction of this longshore movement will depend on which series of waves is dominant, and over a season there may be a pronounced movement of sand back and forth along a beach. The most conspicuous changes, however, are those on the beach profile caused by the intensity of wave action. During periods of heavy wave action the beach is steepened, and consequently narrowed, while during periods of moderate seas the profile may be gradual and the beach correspondingly broader. Such effects are, of course, not noticeable on rocky shores except for the piling of sand around the bases of rocks where there is a nearby source of sand for the waves to work upon. When this happens, collecting may not be so good for the animals that live in crevices and under rocks, but conspicuous animals like sea urchins and abalones may be found perched on higher rocks, forced upward by the encroaching sand.

TIDES

The most characteristic thing about the seashore is the tides, the twice daily movement of water back and forth. In some parts of the world, as at Wellington, New Zealand, this movement is in two almost equal daily rises and falls; in other parts of the world there may be only one rise and fall of the tide in a day. Here on our coast there is a large difference between the two highs and lows, with the result that we have one low-low tide, one high-high tide, and one high-low and one low-high tide almost every day. The tides go through a cycle of maximum and minimum differences in height every 14 days, so that there are two periods of extreme tides every lunar month of 28 days. In regions where these tides coincide with the full and dark of the moon, these extreme tides are called springs; the tides of minimum range, associated with the quarters of the moon, are called neaps. To call a low tide a neap tide is not correct, since the exact meaning of the term is the level at which high water is lowest. During such periods the tides are usually not low enough to expose the lower zones. The spring tides are conversely the tides of highest and lowest levels. As if this were not complicated enough, we must point out that our tides are more properly known as tropic and equatorial or declinational

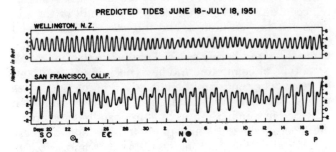

Tides at Wellington, N. Z., and San Francisco

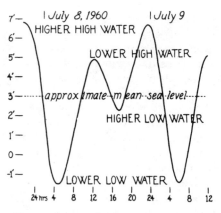

Characteristics of tide at San Francisco

tides, because the periods of maximum and minimum ranges coincide more closely with the height of the moon in relation to the celestial equator than with her phases. The tropic tides are those of maximum range and correspond to the springs, and the equatorials are the counterparts of neaps.

The causes of tides and their characteristics from one place to the next are a complicated subject. The primary tidal force is the moon, which pulls both water and earth toward it, with the result that the tide is high on the other side of the earth from the moon at the same time. Thus the system of tide, moon, and earth is slightly eccentric. Other factors such as the pull of the sun must also be considered, and the exact nature of tidal forces is so complex that enormous machines have been devised for predicting tides. Tide-predicting machines are a type of computer, and have been in use for about 80 years. The times and heights given in the tide tables published by the Coast and Geodetic Survey, and often provided in summary form by ship chandlers and sporting goods concerns, are predicted by one of these machines in Washington, D. C. As it is impossible to predict the winds, or the amount of sand that may be piled up by waves from day to day, these predictions are not always accurate. The levels given in the tide tables are somewhat artificial, as they are based on an average of low waters. For the San Francisco Bay region, this level or datum is that determined for Fort Point. The zero of the tide table is the zero of this datum. It is actually about 3 feet below the mean level of the sea, and a "minus" tide of –0.5 is therefore more like three and a half feet below the mean sea level (or average height of the tide) rather than only six inches below, as some people think when reading the tide zero of the tables.

SEA WATER

Since water is not the environment in which we live, we often fail to realize just what water may mean for the plants and animals that live in it, and as far as the sea is concerned, what the chemicals of sea water mean to life. The most obvious thing about the sea is that it is water. Water is a much denser medium than air, some 775 times as dense. With such external support, few marine plants have any rigidity and the seaweeds are mostly limp things that cannot support their own weight at low tide. Both jellyfish and whales are creatures that can survive only under water, and both die when stranded on the beach—partly because they both lack adequate skeletal structure to maintain their body shape in the air. It is also possible for the creatures of the sea to carry much heavier skeletons about with them than they could on land, so we find snails with heavy shells and thickly armored crabs and lobsters.

The chemical composition of sea water makes it possible for most of the organisms of the sea to manage with simpler body chemistry than those of land and fresh water, whose principal physiological concerns (other than reproduction) involve the acquisition and retention of essential chemical substances and the prevention of water loss. Sea water is about 96.5% water; the remaining 3.5% is a mixture of every element known on earth, but for the most part it is a solution of certain common salts—the chlorides and sulfates of sodium, magnesium, and calcium.

TABLE 1. THE COMPOSITION OF SEA WATER

Elements, mg./liter (parts per million)		Ions, ‰ (parts per thousand at a salinity of 34.48‰, or 3.48%)	
Oxygen	857,000		
Hydrogen	108,000		
Chlorine	19,000	Cl^-	18.97
Sodium	10,500	Na^+	10.55
Magnesium	1,300	Mg^{++}	1.27
Sulfur	900	$SO_4^=$	2.64
Calcium	400	Ca^{++}	0.40
Potassium	380	K^+	0.38
Bromine	65	Br^-	0.06
Carbon	28	HCO_3^-	0.11
		$CO_3^=$	0.01
Strontium	8.0	Sr^{++}	0.01
Boron	4.8	H_3BO_3	0.02
Silicon	3.0		
Fluorine	1.3	F^-	0.001

Some trace elements, in mg./l: Iron, 0.01; Uranium, 0.003; Silver, 0.0003; Gold, 0.000004; Radium, 0.00000000003.

The proportions of these common salts are so constant in the sea that it is possible to determine the total concentration (or salinity) of sea water by analyzing for chloride alone. Because of the comparatively small amounts involved, and the need for critical accuracy, it is simpler to treat these concentrations in terms of parts per thousand rather than per hundred, so the usual way of referring to the chemicals of sea water is with the symbol ‰, i.e., the salinity of sea water is 35‰. The total concentration of sea water varies from ocean to

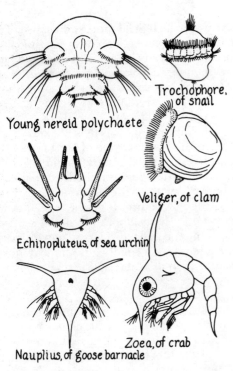

Young nereid polychaete

Trochophore, of snail

Veliger, of clam

Echinopluteus, of sea urchin

Zoea, of crab

Nauplius, of goose barnacle

Some common larval types (greatly enlarged)

ocean but the proportions still remain essentially the same. Thus the Atlantic Ocean has an average salinity of 35‰, the Pacific about 34‰.

So many basically different kinds of life live in sea water, and so many of them resemble in one way or another the oldest fossils, that we often think of sea water as the basic solution necessary for life. It is certainly true that much of evolution is concerned with the development of ways in which animals handle the problem of maintaining an internal balance of salts, a process known as osmoregulation. Many animals of the sea have internal body fluids only slightly different from sea water, and consequently they devote little food or energy to this physiological process. Because of the supply of salts in sea water, it is also possible for many marine plants and animals to release small yolkless eggs whose subsequent development demands an outside source of supply. Few fresh water organisms have such eggs. Many marine organisms go through several different stages of development from these small yolkless eggs; often the larval stages, as they are known, are very different from the adults. Some of these, when first discovered, were considered separate animals and to this day bear names that once implied a separate entity; indeed, the early way of life of these stages is often as different as their structure. It might be said that one of the characteristic things about life in the sea is the variety and abundance of these larval stages. Not all marine animals have such small eggs and elaborate larval stages; many, such as squid and octopus, have heavily yolked eggs and the young hatch from them as miniature adults.

Another advantage of water as an environment, and of sea water in particular, is the manner in which all sorts of food material can be carried about in suspension. As a result, there is in the sea a host of animals that feed by trapping this fine material in one way or another. Many worms and all but a few clams have fine cilia that, by their continuous beating action, set up currents along tentacles, grooves, or flat surfaces that bring food particles into contact with fine, sieve-like sheets of mucus. Others simply grab small particles with various fishing devices like the feet of barnacles. Some of these food gathering arrangements are very efficient: it is such efficiency that makes the mussel poisonous in summer time by the concentration of minute, poisonous algae from the sea water. Other mechanisms in marine animals may be even more efficient at concentrating substances from the sea. Sea squirts, for example, may concentrate vanadium within their tissues to some 280,000 times that in the water itself. Such chemical virtuosity in marine animals may well be one of the principal problems in the atomic age, since we shall have to take great care with what we dump in the sea and how we prevent it from being taken up by sea creatures.

THE ECONOMY OF THE SEA

Two most frequently asked questions about sea life are "What is it good for?" and "How much food can we expect from the sea?" The first question, as crudely put, is one that does not occur either to a religious person or to a naturalist. The religious person may be content with his inadequacy to understand the Divine Plan, while the naturalist suspects that every creature has some function in the natural system. Nobody knows, really, how much food we may expect from the sea for the growing human population, but the answer ultimately depends on our understanding of what the creatures of the sea are "good for." Life is pretty much a process of juggling carbon atoms back and forth with the aid of sunlight. It is often said that the beginning of this process, the fixation of carbon by plants in a form that may be utilized by animals, is very inefficient. We are not so sure. One of the most significant discoveries of the recent bomb tests was not that radioactive materials could become incorporated into organic tissues, but the speed of the process and the rapid transfer of isotopes from one group of animals to another. Thus it appears that whatever the efficiency of nature's process of handling carbon, the whole business proceeds at a very rapid rate and at a surprisingly high level of turnover. Massive withdrawals of living substances of the sea by man, without any thought of replacement, may not be feasible. We cannot take billions of dollars from the treasury without some sort of readjustment, yet we have taken billions of pounds of organic matter from the sea in a short time. If man expects to maintain his increasing numbers on this earth, he must give up his wasteful procedure of removing his remains and metabolic waste products from the cycle by sanitation processes that are essentially anti-ecological.

The begining of the process in the sea is the fixation of carbon as carbohydrates by plants. In this initial step, only about 0.2% of the energy from the sun is converted. Much of this loss is due to reflection from the surface of the ocean and because not all wave lengths of sunlight can be utilized by plants in the process of photosynthesis. In the open sea the key organisms in this process are minute, single-celled plants called diatoms (which, together with other plant-like forms, make up the phytoplankton). Diatoms, so named because they have little silicate shells, or frustules, in two parts, compose a phylum of plants. They look like little pill-boxes, needles, chains of spiny capsules, stars, or spindles. They occur so abundantly at times that the water is greenish or brown with them. The diatoms are far more significant in the economy of the sea than the large seaweeds along the shore. Some diatoms form colonies in thin tubes resembling soft, brown or greenish fur, or brown scum on rocks and large seaweeds; such

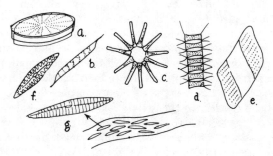

Some representative diatoms. a: *Coscinodiscus;* b: *Rhizoso-lenia;* c: *Astrionella* (a star-shaped colony); d: *Chaetoceras* (a string of individuals); e: *Isthmia* (a large, purse-shaped bottom type); f: *Navicula,* and g: *Schizonema* (spindle-shaped forms often living in tubes and forming fuzzy colonies).

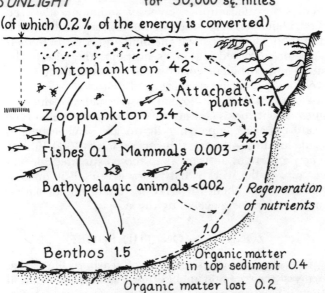

Annual organic budget, in
millions of tons (dry weight)
SUNLIGHT for 30,000 sq. miles
(of which 0.2% of the energy is converted)

Phytoplankton 42

Attached plants 1.7

Zooplankton 3.4

42.3

Fishes 0.1   Mammals 0.003

Bathypelagic animals <0.02

Regeneration of nutrients

1.0

Benthos 1.5

Organic matter in top sediment 0.4

Organic matter lost 0.2

The organic budget off southern California (values from
K. O. Emery, 1960)

shore or littoral diatoms are an important source of food
for limpets, periwinkles, and other "grazing" animals.

The oceanic diatoms constitute the "grass" of the sea,
and are fed upon by young fishes and hosts of lesser
animals (zooplankton). Some of the latter, as they
grow larger, turn to eating their smaller kindred or creatures of other kinds. In ecological language, the diatoms
are called the "producers," and the grazers, the "primary
consumers." The next step is that of the secondary consumers or predators. Not all diatoms are eaten, nor are
all animals eaten by other animals. Many sink or die
and are consumed by organisms on the bottom, the

"reducers" and "transformers." Most organic life is recycled in some manner, but a certain amount of it becomes locked in the sediment for geological periods. In the nutritious upper layer of sediment, however, there is another large group of animals, especially worms and echinoderms, that eat the mud and contribute their share of reworked matter as nutrients that rise to the surface by turbulence or upwelling to contribute to the well-being of succeeding crops of diatoms.

We are still unable to make more than an educated guess about the magnitude of this organic cycle in the sea. In the accompanying figure are some estimates made for the southern California region by K. O. Emery. The proportions are similar to those estimated for other parts of the world; that is, for every 40–50 units of plant material, about 10% is converted to animal matter, and over 90% is recycled by the system.

ZONATION ON THE SHORE

One of the obvious features of seashore life is that many of the common animals observed tend to occur at certain levels or zones. This zonal arrangement, while associated with tidal levels, may be altered by wave action, and is less obvious on gently sloping beaches than on vertical rock faces. Many of the common intertidal animals live nowhere else and probably require a certain amount of exposure to flourish (or, conversely, this escape from predation by animals that cannot stand exposure may give these animals a survival value). Many of the seaweeds also occur within fairly narrow limits, and from their occurrence we can characterize some of the zones. The late E. F. Ricketts designated the major zones on the Pacific Coast by number, and this has been generally followed by students since. These are the large numbers, 1–2–3–4, indicated on the diagram of zonation. Alongside these zones the tidal heights, both actual and according to tidal data, have

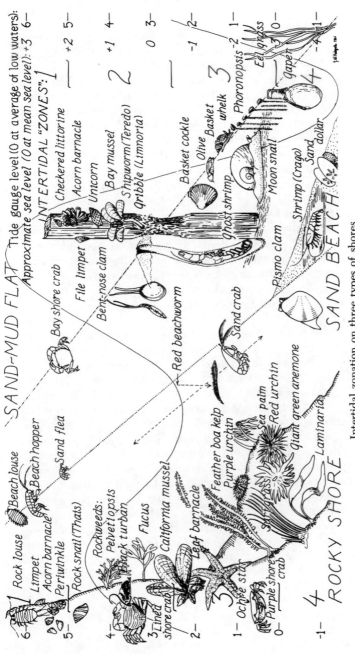

Intertidal zonation on three types of shores

been indicated at the right. Similar zonal arrangements occur on all temperate ocean shores.

The uppermost zone, often called the spray zone or supralittoral, is the region where we find small white barnacles (*Balanus glandula*), and smaller brown barnacles (*Chthamalus dalli*), the periwinkles or littorines (*Littorina planaxis*, and lower down, *L. scutulata*), and the active, scurrying Rock Louse (*Ligia occidentalis*). Farther north may be found a much larger isopod (*Ligia pallasi*, which overlaps *L. occidentalis* in our area). No conspicuous seaweeds occur in this zone, although there are often green, turf-like growths of some species of *Enteromorpha* and thin films of smaller kinds. On sandy shores this zone is characterized by the occurrence of the large Beach Hoppers (*Orchestoidea californiana* and *O. corniculata*) and the smaller Beach Fleas (*Orchestia traskiana*). These animals are also found on some bay shores.

The second zone, or rockweed zone, is characterized at its upper limits by tufts of greenish brown, rather stiff algae of the genera *Pelvetiopsis* and *Pelvetia* (longer or stringier), and a bit lower down by *Fucus*, which is broader and flatter and more olive green than brown. Among these weeds may be found the young littorines and other snails. The common Rock Snail (*Thais emarginata*) of this region, often wandering higher up, is a predaceous snail related distantly to the famous purples. Another common snail, occurring slightly lower, is the Black Turban (*Tegula funebralis*). The conspicuous active animal of this zone is the Lined Shore Crab (*Pachygrapsus crassipes*). On bay shores the place of this crab is taken by the Bay Crab (*Hemigrapsus oregonensis*). On bay flats of this zone may often be seen little villages of conical mounds, marking the sites of burrows of the pinkish Ghost Shrimp (*Callianassa californiensis*). Lower down, in muddy situations, there is a bluish relative (*Upogebia pugettensis*). Various clams live in this zone as well.

The third zone, just below mean sea level to the upper limit of the lowest tides (approximately tide gauge zero) is the "midlittoral zone," frequented by a host of creatures. Here is where the California Mussel (*Mytilus californianus*) and the large Leaf Barnacle (*Pollicipes polymerus*) abound. One can see, on shores where wave action is heavy, how this zone or band of mussels and leaf barnacles widens out toward the surf. In the lower part of the zone on rocky shores we find the Purple Shore Crab (*Hemigrapsus nudus*) and the Brown Turban (*Tegula brunnea*) a taller, heavier relative of the Black Turban. That most characteristic denizen of our rocky coasts, the Ochre Star (*Pisaster ochraceus*) is common here but may stray much higher and is often found feeding on barnacles well up on the shore. In this zone, sometimes fairly high up on isolated rocks, there are carpets of sea anemones. At low tides these look like squishy beds of sandy gravel and bits of shell, because of this animal's habit of attaching these materials to its outer surface. This is the Aggregated Sea Anemone (*Anthopleura elegantissima*). Sometimes at the same level, but more abundant lower, is the Giant Green Anemone (*Anthopleura xanthogrammica*).

On sandy beaches such zonation is less pronounced, but in this general region there occurs a brilliant red worm (*Pectinophelia*) some 12 or 18 inches below the surface. The common Sand Crab (*Emerita analoga*) is generally found somewhere in this third zone, but moves up and down with the tide to a certain extent; it does not occur in very loose sand, however. On bay shores of sandy mud we find various predaceous snails, especially the Moon Snail (*Polinices lewisi*), the Basket Whelk (*Nassarius fossatus*), and a detritus feeder, the Purple Olive (*Olivella biplicata*). In the lower part of the zone, but sometimes extending well above tide zero, may be found dense stands of the interesting, worm-like creature, *Phoronopsis harmeri*. This organism, more closely related to brachiopods and bryozoans than to the worms it resembles, builds a vertical tube of sand grains. On rocky shores the lower limit of this zone is marked by the holdfasts or attachment structures of the Feather Boa Kelp (*Egregia menziesi*), a long, strap-like seaweed with small blades and float bladders like large olives.

The lowest zone, Zone 4 or "infralittoral," is the part of the shore exposed only at the lowest tides. This is the zone on rocky shores of the green Surf Grass (*Phyllospadix*) and the flat-bladed brown kelps of the genus *Laminaria*. On wave-swept rocks we find the large Red Urchin (*Strongylocentrotus franciscanus*) and the Palm Tree Kelp (*Postelsia palmaeformis*). The smaller Purple Urchin (*Strongylocentrotus purpuratus*) lives somewhat nearer shore and may occur up into Zone 3. This lowest zone is the home of a host of smaller creatures, of encrusting sponges, hydroids, bryozoans, and all sorts of small, scrambling creatures under rocks and in fissures. Many of these creatures occur higher up in sheltered places such as the cracks between rocks on jetties and in natural caves. On sandy shores (south of Santa Cruz) we find Pismo Clams (*Tivela stultorum*) and almost everywhere the Gray Shrimp (*Crago*) in the swash pools. Sand dollars usually live below the lowest tide but may occasionally be found at low tide. On bay shores of sandy mud this is the habitat of clams par excellence, especially the Gaper (*Tresus nuttalli*). In sheltered areas there may be extensive meadows of the ribbon-like Eel Grass (*Zostera marina*), which is rooted below the lowest tide level.

A SYNOPSIS OF COMMON SEASHORE LIFE

It is hoped that this part of the book will introduce the reader to many of the most common animals of the local sea and bay shores. There are several hundred different kinds of larger animals in this area (to say nothing of those visible only under high magnifications), and in some groups identification is not an easy task, even for experts. It must be remembered that even for those animals specifically mentioned, this cannot be a very complete introduction; many more, for which we do not have space to consider, may be found by a beginner or a lucky beachcomber on his first few trips to the shore. For many of the creatures of the sea we know nothing more than their names, but the names do imply certain zoological relationships. Accordingly, we have provided some information about the zoology of our fauna. From these beginnings the reader can proceed to tackle some of the more advanced books listed in the References at the back of this book.

We do not know the activities of many of the creatures to which we can give names, and being able to recognize an animal by name is only the beginning of knowledge. We have no common or vernacular names for many of our most abundant seashore animals, so the reader must put up with these strange, italicized words. Do not be afraid to pronounce them; nobody now living knows what the Greeks and Romans really sounded like, and it has become a bit of a joke at international meetings that the scientific names are harder to follow than the language of the speaker. Although some people seem to think we should make up common names for those animals that have none, such names are not only erroneously reassuring but can also be misleading.

We do ask, however, that the term "species" be properly used. This word is both singular and plural; there is no such thing as a "specie" of plant or animal. When we are not sure or do not know the name of an organism, we often refer to it as "sp."; thus, *Balanus* sp. When several species may be involved, we indicate this by the expression "spp." after the genus.

To begin with, it is not always easy to tell a plant from an animal on the seashore, and a hand lens of about 7 or 10 power is essential. However, if you are looking at some growth from the underside of a rock or from a deep fissure or cave, it is probably not a plant. The plants of the seashore are green, brown, black, or various shades of red from purple to pink. They do not have any fine structure of sculpturing, small holes, or spaces or other uneven texture visible with a hand lens. One genus of seaweeds, the red algae *Gigartina* spp., has prominent finger-like or spur-like tubercles on the surface of the broad "leaf" (properly, thallus), but these are otherwise easily recognizable as seaweeds, and the common species, *Gigartina corymbifera*, has a thallus often exceeding one foot in area.

In fact, texture, once learned, is the first sure guide to distinguish the larger marine plants from animals (of course this cannot apply to the microscopic, unicellular things, and many experts still argue about some of these). There are some common organisms which may at the outset cause confusion. The thin, pink crust that seems to be laid down in sheets or layers, but sometimes with lumpy growths in it, on rocks and various seashells, is an encrusting red alga, a type of *Lithothamnion*. Other red algae grow in small bushy tufts like bryozoans, but are hard and gritty and seem to be made up of small jointed parts—these are the coralline algae such as *Corallina* and *Bossea*. The grayish-brown, fleshy, flat growth resembling a seaweed, with lobes about three inches long, is a bryozoan, *Flustrella*. It is never green or seaweed-brown, and when looked at with a hand lens it shows many irregular compartments with little forked brown structures suggesting tiny deer antlers scattered over the surface.

a: *Corallina gracilis;* b: *Flustrella corniculata* (both × 1/5).

Having made the assumption that the specimen in hand is an invertebrate animal (we assume that fish, birds, and mammals are easily recognized as such), we can proceed somewhat as follows.

1. **Either:**
   a. The specimen forms sheets, crusts, or lumps on rocks or piling or larger animals, often of bright colors. This group includes examples of sponges, a hydrocoral, bryozoans, and compound ascidians. Go to number 2
   b. Or, it is attached but not encrusting, forming bushy, feathery, or bristly growths of various types; usually white, yellowish, brown, or gray. Sometimes these are conspicuous feathery or bushy tufts. Very fine brown felt or mossy tufts may be colonial diatoms. Hydroids and bryozoans, for the most part . . 4

Or:
   c. The animal, if attached, arises from a stalk or base and is clearly recognizable as a sea anemone, barnacle, vaselike sponge, or a not too symmetrical leathery or gelatinous object; *or*, it is some sort of worm living in a tube attached to rocks . . . 6
   d. Or, it is either not attached but is free swimming or crawling or running; or, if attached, is obviously some sort of clam or oyster: Most of the Metazoa 11

2. a. Thick, slippery, fleshy lumps or masses; yellowish gray, reddish, orange, lavender, or pink; smooth, with yellowish or orange spots of the small individuals (zooids) scattered through the substance . . . . Chordata: Compound ascidians (p. 127)
   b. Never with such structures scattered in a fleshy matrix 3

3. a. Thin or spongy crusts (rarely fleshy masses) with conspicuous crater-like holes over the surface, and more numerous but much smaller holes between them; often bright red, orange, or lavender . . . . Porifera: Sponges (p. 47)

[31]

A bright purple, encrusting organism with jagged or star-like openings is a hydrocoral, *Allopora porphyra* (common at Monterey).

b. Crusts that are hard to the touch, seldom very thick, often lacy or reticulated in appearance; usually whitish, gray, light salmon, or pink; sometimes raised up from rock or other subsurface . . . . . .
. . . . Bryozoa (p. 119)

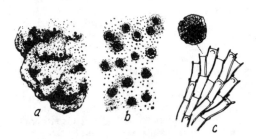

a: An encrusting sponge; b: *Allopora porphyra,* a hydrocoral; c: *Membranipora,* a bryozoan (habit sketches × 1).

4. a. Forms a growth resembling tubes or straws packed closely together, about one to two inches high, soft to the touch, dirty white. A calcareous sponge . .
. . . . *Leucosolenia eleanor* (p. 48)
Very small white tubes of lime, densely packed, are of a polychaete, *Salmacina.*

b. Bushy, feathery, or fern-like growths, or with the appearance of coarse fuzz or minute stubble on rocks 5

5. a. Forms small bushes, whitish or pinkish, with minute pattern of darker spots along entire length of stalks; not symmetrically branched like ferns or feathers
. . . . Bryozoa: *Bugula* spp. (p. 119)

b. Individuals not easily seen along stalks; colonies may be simple stalks or dense, bushy growths or various types of feathery, open growths; usually white or yellowish . . . Coelenterata: Hydrozoa (p. 50)
Small, greenish or brownish, fuzzy colonies at bases of seaweeds are not animals but colonial diatoms.

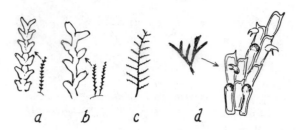

Hydroids (× 1, with details enlarged): a: *Sertularia;*
b: *Sertularella;* c: *Abietinaria;* d: Bryozoan: *Bugula.*

6. a. Attached animals not protected by plates, shells, or
    tubes 8
  b. Sedentary, attached, protected by plates, shells, or
    tubes 7

7. a. Protected by a series of overlapping plates, with
    paired plates forming a door which can be tightly
    closed, attached by flat base or stiff fleshy stalk . .
    . . . . . . Arthropoda: Barnacles (p. 77)
  b. Encased in a tube, which may be white, cemented
    for most of its length on a rock *(Serpula)* or as a
    small tight spiral perhaps 1/16″ to 1/10″ across
    (Spirorbis); or as dense, erect, dingy gray tubes form-
    ing conspicuous coral-like lumps *(Mercierella, Dode-*
    caceria) . Annelida: Tubicolous polychaetes (p. 58)

8. a. Vase or finger-like structures without tentacles or
    obvious symmetry, usually in groups hanging from
    ledges or under rocks 9
  b. Irregular in shape but with two prominent openings,
    or regular, radially (like a wheel) symmetrical, with
    tentacles 10

9. a. White, slender, vase-like structures about one and a
    half inches long with a single opening at apex; a
    calcareous sponge . . . *Rhabdodermella nuttingi*
  b. Finger-like, translucent individuals about two inches
    long, with bright pink internal structure, in clusters
    joined together at bases. A social ascidian . . .
    . . . . *Clavelina huntsmani*

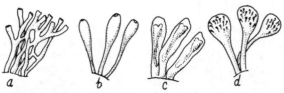

a: *Leucosolenia eleanor;* b: *Rhabdodermella nuttingi;*
c: *Clavelina huntsmani;* d: *Distaplia* sp. (all × 1).

10. a. Small to large, with pronounced radial symmetry
and with a single central opening . . . . . .
. . Coelenterata: Sea anemones and corals (p. 53)
b. With two prominent openings, one of which may be
down on the side; stalked, leathery, reddish *(Styela
montereyensis)*; yellowish or greenish, tough, irregular in shape *(Ascidia ceratodes)*; thin, grayish or
greenish, with both apertures at end, on piling *(Ciona
intestinalis)*; or of various globular or lumpy shapes
and textures. Sea squirts . . . .
. . . . Chordata, Ascidians (p. 128)

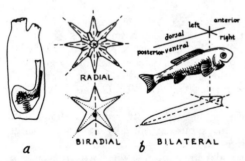

a:*Ciona intestinalis* × 1/3; b: Types of symmetry as exemplified
by a sea anemone (radial), sea star (biradial), fish and flatworm
(bilateral)

11. a. Symmetry that of a wheel (radial) or of a five-rayed
star, so that there may be two halves (biradial) . 12
b. Symmetry of two equal sides (bilateral), which may
be obscured by a coiled shell; or worm or slug-like
with one end developed into a bushy tuft or apparently radial pattern of tentacles or gills . . . 13

[34]

12. a. With tough, spiny skin; rays usually in fives, but sometimes in six or over 20; or with small central disk and five flexible rays, or flattened or squatly globe-shaped, covered with spines. Sea stars, serpent stars, urchins . . . . . Echinodermata (p. 121)
  b. Soft, jelly-like, bell- or mushroom-shaped with tentacles around margin (sometimes a foot or more in diameter). Jellyfish . Coelenterata: Medusae (p. 48)

13. a. Segmented, worm-like, with lateral lobes or processes (parapodia) or with conspicuous legs 14
  b. Not conspicuously segmented or worm-like. Clams, snails, slugs, etc. 15

14. a. With jointed legs (crabs, shrimp, insects, etc.) . .
    . . . . Arthropoda (p. 64)
  b. Without such legs; worms with obvious segmentation and lateral structures (parapodia), and conspicuous bristles, with various head tentacles and reversible jaws (*Polychaeta errantia*); or burrowing forms with reduced parapodia, no jaws, and various gill-like processes (filaments, tufts, etc. for feeding and respiration), or living in tubes of parchment-like or gelatinous consistency with embedded sand grains; bearing a crown of tentacles. Bristle worms . . .
    . . . . Annelida: Polychaeta (p. 59)

15. a. For all animals that are obviously molluscs, or appear to be so, including snails, sea slugs, chitons, clams, brachiopods, and for various slug-like animals go to 18
    (For squids and octopuses, proceed directly to p. 118)
  b. We are now left with a host of worm-like creatures of various types and shapes, whose real differences require some information about their insides. Several of them have structures which they pull inside when disturbed; hence their nature may be uncertain unless they are seen in a tide pool or aquarium in an expanded state. Some of these are considered under 19
    This leaves us with various unsegmented small to large, thread-, string-, and leaf-like worms . . 16

[35]

and two other kinds of worms found on bay flats: it is unsafe, for purposes of basic identification, to characterize animals by the places in which they are found, but for this limited area we can dispose of two common worms living in permanent burrows. The first of these is the phoronid, *Phoronopsis harmeri,* that builds vertical tubes of sand grains about a third the diameter of a pencil; on sandy flats just below mid-tide level .   .   .   .   (p. 120) The worm is slender, with red blood and a green plume of tentacles conspicuous in shallow pools. On exposed surfaces the phoronid retracts into its tube, leaving a small hole to mark its presence. The other is the Fat Innkeeper, the echiurid, *Urechis caupo,* living in U-shaped burrows .   .   .   .   (p. 62) The back door of the burrow is a hole less than half an inch in diameter, surrounded by rod-like fecal pellets resembling the chocolate drops used for decorating cakes. The animal itself lives two or three feet below the surface and resembles, among other things, a flesh-colored, peristaltic sausage.

16. a. Worms, long, round, or elliptical in cross sections   .
.   .   .   .   17

b. Flattened, leaf-like worms gliding closely over surfaces. Some of these are brightly colored, striped, or mottled. Flatworms .   .   .   .
.   .   .   .   .   Platyhelminthes: Turbellaria (p. 56) An opisthobranch mollusc, *Elysia hedgpethi,* green with small blue spots, occurs on green seaweed in bay flats; at first glance may be confused with a large flatworm, but the rolled structure of the head tentacles clearly separates it from flatworms, some of which have a pair of flat tentacles.

a: A flatworm, *Leptoplana;* b: A mollusc, *Elysia hedgpethi* (both × 2).

17. a. Thread-like worms, circular in cross section, mostly microscopic, some visible with hand lens, white or colorless, with a writhing, spring-like motion. Roundworms . . . . Nematoda
   b. String-like, rubbery, elongate worms, elliptical in cross-section, usually pigmented, somewhat darker above, some banded with contrasting colors, capable of elongation, and with an eversible proboscis which the worm uses to capture prey. Ribbon worms . . . . Nemertea (p. 57)

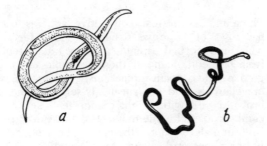

a: A nematode ($\times$ 100); b: *Emplectonema gracilis*, a nemertean ($\times$ 1/2).

18. a. Without shells or hard covering, slug- or thickly worm-like, with or without projections, spurs, papillae, or retractible bushy processes at one end or the other, often brightly colored but not always so . . 19
   b. With shells 21

19. a. The animal, when placed in water, glides along on its lower surface and has two pairs of "tentacles" or sensory structures at the leading end. The surface may be smooth or adorned with branched or unbranched growth. Sea slugs . . . . Mollusca: Opisthobranchia (p. 104)
   There are two common types of sea slugs: the nudibranchs, with prominent processes often regularly arranged along the back (eolids), or with a prominent retractible rosette of gills near the hind end (dorids); and the tectibranchs, smooth-surfaced with

the gill beneath a flap on the right side. The commonest example of a tectibranch is the eel grass slug, *Phyllaplysia zostericola,* green with narrow black stripes. A possibly confusing animal resembling an orange dorid, or a chiton when retracted, but much less active than either, is a peculiar sea cucumber, *Psolus chitinoides.*

b. The animals, if placed in water, do not move actively, or if they do, it is by writhing or changing shape, and they do not show well-defined directional movement 20

20. a. The animal is not markedly active, adheres to rocks, has rows of adhesive structures (tube feet), and when undisturbed expands a bushy tuft of tentacles from one end. Some of these resemble small, black garden slugs, occur gregariously; others are white or yellowish, and one species is several inches long, brownish red with bright orange tentacles. Sea cucumbers . Echinodermata: Holothuroidea (p. 125)

b. The animals do not adhere by tube feet, but may writhe about and change their shape.
This category includes the transparent sea cucumber of sandy mud flats, *Leptosynapta inhaerens,* and the sipunculids or peanut worms (p. 64) which have opaque bodies, white or brownish (often with darker spots).

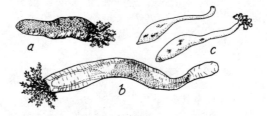

a: *Cucumaria curata* ($\times$ 2/3); b: *Leptosynapta inhaerens* ($\times$ 1); c: *Phascolosoma agassizi* ($\times$ 1/2).

21. a. Shells in pairs. Clams, mussels, oysters .   .   .   .   .
.   .   .   . Mollusca: Pelecypoda (p. 107)
Rarely, brachiopods may be found in this area. These can be distinguished from clams by the presence of the stalk,

[38]

or the hole in the larger (lower) half through which the stalk projects. Our local brachiopods are attached to rocks or the holdfasts of seaweeds. The smaller, separated valve of a brachiopod cannot be distinguished readily from a clam shell by a novice (see p. 121).

b. Shells single, as in snails, or in rows of eight somewhat overlapping plates 22

a: *Terebratalia transversa,* a brachiopod; b: "Butterfly shell," a plate from *Cryptochiton stelleri* (both × 1).

22. a. Snails, sea slugs (some of which, like the common black and white Barrel Shell, *Actaeon,* are shelled), limpets, abalones . Mollusca: Gastropoda (p. 93) Very small, flattened, spiral objects found in beach sands and among detritus at the bases of seaweeds and similar locations are Foraminifera (see p. 46).

b. Slug-like in outline, with a rubbery or leathery girdle surrounding eight plates. Chitons . . . . Mollusca: Amphineura (p. 90) In our largest chiton, *Cryptochiton stelleri,* the plates are completely covered by a heavy, reddish-brown tunic. This animal, which may be a foot long, is called the Gum Boot (some arty people call it Chinese Abalone, but it is inedible, even by Chinese).

SOME ZOOLOGY

The synopsis on the foregoing pages has been designed as a guide for those without a background in zoology, although even for this beginning some formidable words have crept in. We do not classify plants or animals according to their superficial appearance, but by their structure and the manner in which this structure has been developed. This often involves knowledge both of the manner in which the egg divides and of features in the embryo which may not be found in the adult. Obviously some of these things can be determined only by specialists, and the beginner, as well as many zoologists, cannot be certain of the classification of many animals on the basis of their apparent structure.

The major branches of the animal kingdom are called phyla. No one has defined a phylum successfully, and there are still uncertainties about what should be included in these major divisions. Our scheme of classification is simply our sense of order applied to nature, and our sense of what is orderly changes with the times. Old naturalists included almost everything they did not know what else to do with under Vermes, or worms. Today we recognize as many basically different kinds of animals as we consider necessary, and we use the idea of the phylum to include organisms having basic relations of structure, development, and reproduction. According to some schemes of classification, there are thirty or more phyla, while others include only half as many.

There are perhaps three levels or grades of structure into which the phyla are divided (see table 2). The first of these includes the minute creatures usually called Protozoa. Of these, two basically different types seem to be in one way or another related to the rest of the animal kingdom, as will be explained further below.

The protozoans include many small complex animals, characterized principally by their smallness and lack of cells, or, as consisting of but one cell. A number of very different types of organization have been included under this heading, and the two groups related to more complex animals are the Ciliates and the Flagellates, now regarded as phyla, the Ciliata and Rhizoflagellata. The ciliates possess a structure found in most animals, a minute, short, thread- or hair-like structure which beats in one direction. Under the electron microscope the cilia are revealed to have a characteristic structure, a central core of two larger rods circled by nine pairs of smaller rods or fibers. The flagellates have instead a larger, whip-like structure (or several of them) similar to a cilium but more flexible in movement and function. Another group of protozoans, the Rhizopoda or Sarcodina, lack such permanent structures but extend processes of their body as root feet ("rhizopods"); this group includes Amoeba and such characteristic marine organisms as the Foraminifera. Some flagellates have amoeboid stages and the two groups are now combined by some zoologists as Rhizoflagellata.

The similarity of the one-celled individuals in one group of flagellates to the collared cells or choanocytes of sponges (which are found nowhere else in animals), and the peculiar composition of the sponges, suggest that sponges have a completely different order of organization and represent a separate evolution from the great majority of animals. Hence the name Parazoa, which is sometimes used for them. As for the ciliates, it is possible that they represent a line of evolution that has more affinity with the complex organisms we call Metazoa. Indeed, it has been suggested by some zoologists that ciliates may be greatly modified or reduced metazoans.

In some respects the organization of a sponge suggests an elaborate colony of several different types of cells. Some sponges can reassemble themselves after being forced through a very fine screen. No other animal can be treated this way, although it is possible to produce several individuals from an egg of some complex animals by breaking the dividing egg apart at an early stage of division.

The great majority of animals belong to the Metazoa, animals built up of layers of cells that in turn form tissues and organs. If we take a ball and press on one side, we obtain a structure similar to that of a sea anemone. The outer layer of the ball is called the ectoderm, the inner layer the endoderm. Animals constructed this way are called diploblastic. The next stage of complexity

[41]

involves the development of a third layer (the mesoderm) where the pressed-in side of the ball meets the
other side, which may thicken and divide to form a
space between the two original layers. This internal
space, which may be completely closed off, is called a
coelom. We recognize a coelom by its lining of mesoderm (in such an animal as man, this lining is the peri-
toneum), but in many of these three-layered (triploblastic) animals the exact nature of the internal space
is not certain, because we have not been able to follow
its development in satisfactory detail. The Coelenter-

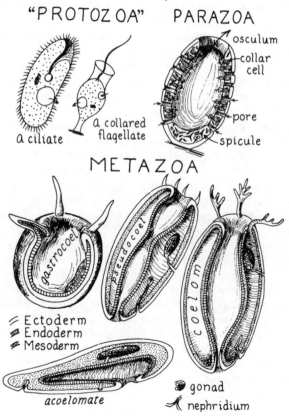

"PROTOZOA" PARAZOA

osculum
collar cell
pore
spicule

a ciliate
a collared flagellate

METAZOA

gastrocoel
pseudocoel
coelom

Ectoderm
Endoderm
Mesoderm

acoelomate

gonad
nephridium

The basic schemes of animal organization

ates have no such space and lack cellular mesoderm, while the flatworms and ribbon worms are solidly packed with this third tissue or mesoderm. Characteristically, muscles and blood vessels are developed from this mesoderm, and in two large groups of animals the blood vessels have expanded to take over most of the internal space—in these, the arthropods and molluscs, the arteries remain as separate vessels while the rest of the space is essentially the veins. In this condition the circulatory system is "open" and the cavity is a "hemocoel"; the "true" coelom is reduced to spaces around the heart or kidneys. Other cavities arise from the space between the original outer and inner layers and may be only partly lined with mesoderm; such a cavity is called a pseudocoel. The coelom is more than an empty space; it provides room for the reproductive organs, and in such animals as the bristle worms its fluids can be compressed by muscular action and the body may be stiffened like a paper snake whistle, thus enabling the worm to move as if it had an internal skeleton.

In most animals with complex inner cavities the structures for handling waste materials are derived from the outer layer of ectoderm; these are primitive kidneys or nephridia. The echinoderms, although triploblastic and with elaborate internal structures derived from mesoderm, have no such excretory structures. In all the animals of which we have adequate knowledge, the nervous system is derived from the outer layer, arising originally as a sensory area on the surface of the embryo.

The opening left in our double-walled ball by the ingrowing endoderm is decreased by growth around it, but it remains the primitive opening, in the sea anemones and flatworms, for taking in food and rejecting unwanted material. The separate mouth and anal openings of more complex animals are developed in two ways. Either the primitive opening (blastopore) is narrowed to a slit, and is then closed except for openings at each end, or a new opening is developed for the

[43]

mouth. These two processes represent the divergent branches of coelomate animals, the Protostomia, which includes the worms, molluscs, and arthropods, and the Deuterostomia, consisting of chordates, echinoderms, and a few smaller groups. Associated with this process of mouth development is the manner in which the embryo is formed by the dividing egg. In the Protostomia the divisions are more uneven and the dividing cells tilt so that the appearance is vaguely spiral. In the other type of cleavage, characteristic of the Deuterostomia, the dividing cells are lined up evenly, and this is called radial cleavage. In many animals, however, cleavage is modified by the presence of yolk, and its nature is assumed from that of closely related groups.

The relationships of the primary layers, and the arrangement of organ systems in the four largest groups of marine animals are presented on Plates 5–8. In these the ectoderm is blue, the endoderm yellow, and the mesoderm red.

TABLE 2. SYNOPSIS OF THE ANIMAL KINGDOM
(NUMBERS APPROXIMATE)

Subkingdom **PROTOZOA**—30,000 species
                Phylum **Rhizoflagellata**
                Phylum **Actinopoda**
                Phylum **Sporozoa**
                Phylum **Cnidosporidia**
                Phylum **Ciliata**
Subkingdom **PARAZOA**   Phylum **Porifera**—4,500 species
Subkingdom **METAZOA** ?Phylum **Mesozoa** (Parasites of octopuses: possibly specialized offshoot of another phylum)
  Grade RADIATA (Radially symmetrical, digestive cavity the only space, no anus)
                Phylum **Coelenterata**—9,000 species, including fossils
                Phylum **Ctenophora**—90 species
  Grade BILATERIA (Bilaterally—or secondarily radially—symmetrical, with mesoderm and usually with secondary body space)
    ACOELOMATES   Phylum **Playthelminthes**—11,000 species

[44]

Phylum **Nemertea**—750 species

(Principal extra-digestive cavity from blastocoel)

Phylum **Entoprocta**—60 species (Small hydroid-like, with U-shaped digestive tract, anus inside ring of tentacles)

Phylum **Priapulida**—6 species (Priapus worms, of uncertain position)

Phylum **Aschelminthes**—12,000 species (Rotifera, nematodes, and some small fry)

Phylum **Acanthocephala**—500 species (Parasites of vertebrates, as adults)

COELOMATES

Schizocoels (Coelom formed by splitting apart of mesoderm, with spiral cleavage of egg, protostomous)

Phylum **Annelida**—7,000 species

Phylum **Sipunculida**—250 species

Phylum **Echiurida**—80 species

Phylum **Onychophora**—12 species (*Peripatus,* exclusively terrestrial)

Phylum **Pentastomida**—70 species (Parasites of lungs of reptiles and mammals)

Phylum **Arthropoda**—900,000 species

Phylum **Mollusca**—80,000 species, including fossils

Phylum **Bryozoa**—3,300 species

Phylum **Brachiopoda**—250 species

Phylum **Phoronida**—12 species

Enterocoels (Coelom formed by inpocketing or pouching of mesoderm, cleavage radial, deuterostomous)

Phylum **Chaetognatha**—40 species

Phylum **Echinoderma**—5,500 species

Phylum **Pogonophora**—45 species (Without digestive system; deep water)

Phylum **Hemichordata**—80 species (Acorn worms, *Balanoglossus,* etc.)

Phylum **Chordata**—70,000 species, mostly fish. (The vertebrates are a specialized branch of an invertebrate phylum)

[45]

PROTOZOA

The unicellular or acellular organisms formerly called protozoa can no longer be considered a natural group, since critical studies reveal differences among them as great as those between echinoderms and molluscs, and several phyla of these small beings are now recognized. The principal groups represented in the sea are the flagellates (together with the Foraminifera), ciliates, and the Actinopoda, which include the Radiolaria. Among the flagellates there is again uncertainty, for some of these are claimed by some botanists because they function as plants, synthesizing their own food material. Such organisms are termed "autotrophic" and include many of the dinoflagellates (which the botanists class as the Division Pyrrophyta). Other dinoflagellates are heterotrophic (eating outside food) and are claimed by some zoologists. One of these, *Noctiluca,* is often common along the shore in summer and may occur so abundantly as to turn the water pink, and at low tide the puddles on the flats may look like pale pink lemonade. As its name implies, *Noctiluca* ("light of the night") is luminescent, and the glowing footprints left by a walker on the beach may be caused by vast numbers of these creatures, since they are less than a millimeter in diameter. One group of dinoflagellates, of which *Gonyaulax polyhedra* is a common local representative, produces an extremely powerful toxin. This may be concentrated by mussels in summer and makes them, and other filter feeding shellfish along the open coast, unsafe for human consumption. Such dinoflagellates may occur in such vast numbers that the water becomes dull yellow or red.

Foraminifera, sea-going relatives of the humble laboratory Amoeba, are abundant on the shore and may be seen with a hand lens. Some look like miniature ammonites with calcareous tests ("shells"); they are found in beach sand and among detritus between stones and around the bases of seaweeds. Two common species are

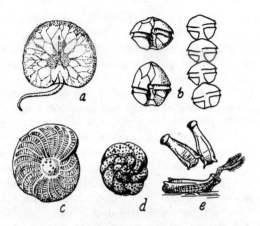

Some protozoans. a: *Noctiluca* (× 20); b: *Gonyaulax polyhedra* (× 200); c: *Elphidium crispum* (× 15); d: *Discorbis patelliformis* (× 15); e: *Valettofolliculina bicornis* (× 25).

Elphidium crispum and *Discorbis patelliformis.* Another common foram, *Gromia oviformis,* is visible to a sharp eye as a minute egg- or ball-like object, completely smooth.

Ciliates (of which *Paramecium* is the best-known example) are abundant everywhere. One group of ciliates, the folliculinids, produce little blue or green bottle-like houses on seaweeds or bits of clean shell. One of the largest of these, *Valletofolliculina bicornis,* is a native of Tomales Bay.

PORIFERA: Sponges

There are at least 45 different species of sponges in our area, but few of them resemble the popular idea of a sponge, and the traditional bath sponge (now rendered obsolete for baths by the ingenuity of the du Pont people) belongs to warmer seas. Most of our sponges are patches, sheets, or lumps of reddish, whitish, or purple material in crevices and on the under surfaces

[47]

of rocks. Sometimes their sponge nature is obvious from the presence of the prominent, irregularly scattered oscula over the surface. While the color of some sponges is diagnostic, final determination of most sponges requires examination of the minute spicules scattered throughout their substance. At the outset it is necessary to determine whether these spicules are composed of lime or silica, which must be done by placing a small piece of sponge in weak acid; if the spicules are calcareous, bubbles will be produced. The most easily identified calcareous sponge in our area is *Rhabdodermella nuttingi*, a graceful white or tan-colored vaselike object about an inch high. Often these sponges occur in patches hanging from the under surface of ledges. Other calcareous sponges are *Leucosolenia eleanor*, which has a superficial structure of joining (anastomosing) tubes, and *Leuconia heathi*, somewhat like *Rhabdodermella* but shorter and rounder.

The sponges with siliceous spicules compose most of the other local species, one of which, the greenish white crumb-of-bread sponge, may be identified by its texture. It occurs somewhat higher than most sponges, often among the mussel beds. One sponge, *Cliona celata*, bores into clam and abalone shells and can be seen as a yellow material in the holes.

Most of our sponges, however, are a bewildering array of brightly colored patches or sheets, with spicules variously shaped like spurs, cockleburs, hooks, collar buttons, and the like, and the determined amateur must equip himself with a microscope and some such introduction as *Light's Manual* to make even a beginning with them.

COELENTERATA
(Plate 5)

There are three classes of Coelenterates: the Hydrozoa, which include many soft, fuzzy, or bushy growths in sheltered places among rocks and on piling, and many of which have small jellyfish for their sexual stage; the Scyphozoa, or large jellyfish; and the Anthozoa, or sea anemones and corals. The Hydrozoa and the anemones are most characteristic of temperate shores, and there are a few large jellyfish in bays but many of them are high seas creatures. The most common growth on bay pilings is the hydroid *Obelia,* so familiar an example in textbooks that many students tacitly assume it to be the "characteristic" coelenterate. Yet, if there is anything to be considered characteristic of coelenterates, it is their diversity. This diversity is especially pronounced in matters of reproduction, and classification is to some extent based on this character. Among the Hydrozoa the polyp or hydroid stage is best developed, and the medusa or jellyfish stages are usually small and shortlived. Many hydroids have no medusa stage in their lives at all. The Scyphozoa are just the opposite, with large, long-lived medusae and, more often than not, no sedentary or polyp stage, although one shore jellyfish, *Haliclystus,* lives like a polyp. The anemones and corals are polyps exclusively, sexually mature and without the vestige of a medusa stage. Many coelenterates are colonial, with numerous individuals joined together by a common stalk. The hydroids produce feathery or bushy colonies, and the corals form massive stony growths in the tropics. Scyphozoan adults and anemones are not colonial but may be very gregarious, and swarms of jellyfish may extend for miles and include millions of individuals.

All coelenterates have nematocysts, often called stinging cells. They are not cells, but are minute structures produced by cells, consisting of a capsule and a long, thread-like process which is everted when the nematocyst functions. This eversion may happen long after the animal is dead, and since there is a toxic substance which may cause a severe rash, it is unsafe to handle even a dead jellyfish carelessly. Too often, the some-

[49]

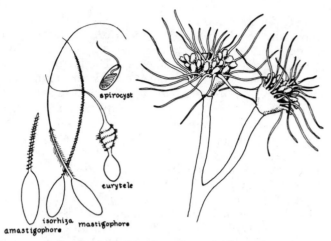

Some nematocysts (greatly enlarged); *Tubularia crocea* (× 3).

what peculiar and restricted nematocysts of the fresh-water *Hydra* are offered as "typical", sometimes illustrated alongside a sea anemone as if they came from the anemone. These structures occur in combinations that vary with each species of coelenterate, and a formidable set of terms for them has accumulated. Some of these are given with the sampling of representative nematocysts in the figure.

HYDROZOA

The most conspicuous hydroid in our waters is *Tubularia crocea*, forming whitish or straw-colored, bushy growths on piling, each stalk topped by a reddish "head" that is actually the individual hydranth, often carrying grapelike bunches of reproductive bodies which are small medusa buds that never break free. Like all coelenterates, *Tubularia* is carnivorous and catches prey with its long slender tentacles.

There are several species of *Obelia*, all of which produce the delicate small medusae so familiar in books.

[50]

a: *Obelia gracilis* (× 1); b: *Obelia longissima;* c: medusae of
Obelia (× 10); d: *Aglaophenia* sp. (habit sketch natural size,
with details enlarged).

Obelia longissima produces the feathery white plumes
on piling, often several inches long and forming side
branches on a longer stalk that may be a foot or more
long. *Obelia gracilis* is a smaller colony with short side
branches of only a few polyps, common on seaweeds in
sheltered places.

One of the most frequently encountered hydroids is
the Ostrich Plume hydroid, *Aglaophenia* sp. Often this
is cast on the beach and holds its structure longer than
most hydroids. It is yellowish or orange, and the thick-
ened, lump-like structures are the reproductive bodies.
Aglaophenia has no medusa stage but hatches the
young out as planula larvae, little ovoid bodies from
which a new hydroid colony is developed.

In contrast to this, one of our abundant small jellyfish, about the size of a demi-tasse cup, is actually a
hydrozoan medusa for which there is not a recognized

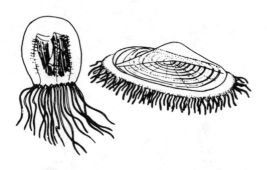

Polyorchis penicillata (× 1/2); *Velella velella* (× 1/2).

hydroid stage. This is *Polyorchis penicillata,* which sometimes occurs by the thousands in bays and quiet waters.

Often in spring and early summer the ocean shores may be covered by windrows of the By-the-Wind-Sailor, *Velella velella,* actually a modified hydrozoan colony with a float and a sail of cellophane-like material. As the animal rots away, nothing is left but this bit of cellophane sail, which may be blown inland for some distance. *Velella* is a member of the Chondrophora, not a siphonophore (like the Portuguese Man-of-War) as many classifications would have it.

Scyphozoa: Jellyfish

The Moon Jelly, *Aurellia aurita,* up to about a foot in diameter, is a world-wide species found in bays and near-shore waters; it is easily recognized because of its comparatively flat, dish-like bell and simple lobes trailing from its mouth. The larger *Chrysaora melanaster* has conspicuous brown stripes on the bell and twenty-four brown to reddish tentacles around the margin of the bell. It is usually seen stranded in a tide pool or on the beach and may be dangerous to allergy-prone people.

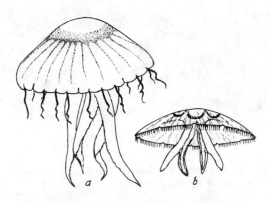

a: *Chrysaora melanaster;* b: *Aurellia aurita* (both × 1/15).

ANTHOZOA: Sea Anemones and Corals

Two anemones are among the most characteristic members of our shore fauna. The first of these may not be observed as such by a casual visitor, as it occurs at mid-tide or above in extensive colonies that form squishy sheets covered with bits of shell and sand. This is the Aggregated Anemone, *Anthopleura elegantissima.* Usually the tips of the tentacles have a pink to violet tinge when expanded. Its larger relative, the Giant Green Anemone, *Anthopleura xanthogrammica,* occurs as separate individuals at lower levels and may be almost a foot in diameter. In sheltered places, such as caves or narrow passageways between rocks, these may occur close together but not in sheets on exposed rocks. Where exposed to light, the body or column of this anemone and its tentacles are green. In darker places it may be almost white. The green color is from symbiotic algae in its tissues.

A third species of this genus, *Anthopleura artemisia,* is a burrowing anemone, attached by its base to a rock or bit of shell several inches below the surface. Its tentacles may be tinted with orange or violet. It is common

a: *Metridium senile;* b: *Epiactis prolifera;* c: *Anthopleura xanthogrammica* (all less than × 1/2).

on bay flats but may also be found in sand on the ocean shore as well. The column is not brightly colored, and the warts are prominent only on the upper half of the column.

A small anemone, never much more than about three quarters of an inch across, is frequently found on sea-weeds and rocks, usually with young anemones adhering to its sides. The base of this anemone has short stripes of darker or lighter color, while the column may be brownish, green, or reddish. This is the Proliferating Anemone, *Epiactis prolifera.*

In the Monterey region, and rarer farther north, there is a small anemone that occurs in several bright colors (red, orange, or lavender) with white tentacles bearing knobs at the tips. This anemone, *Corynactis californica,* is more closely related to corals than to the common shore anemones.

Anemones of a solid bright red, or with red and green columns, belong to the genus *Tealia.* The cherry red one, sometimes seen at lowest tide levels, is *Tealia lofotensis;* the other is *Tealia crassicornis.*

On piling in the bays a large white, pale salmon, or brown anemone is common. This is the Plumose Anemone, *Metridium senile,* a widely distributed species in Europe and America.

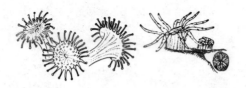

Corynactis californica; Balanophyllia elegans (both × 1).

A small anemone is often abundant on rocks, oyster shell, and piling in the bays, obviously tolerant of muddy conditions. This is *Haliplanella luciae,* with collorless or pale green tentacles and a green column with dull orange stripes. No other local anemone has this pattern.

Coral reefs, which excite the imagination and interest of every naturalist, are far from the shores of the Bay region. They require the clear, warm waters of the tropics and they cannot exist on western shores where upwelling occurs. Not all corals, however, are reef forming, and we do have a small solitary coral, *Balanophyllia elegans,* whose bright orange polyp can be seen by alert observers in crevices and crannies at low tide. It looks like a small orange sea anemone, but when touched it retracts within a hard cup that reveals its coral nature.

CTENOPHORA: Comb Jellies

The comb jellies comprise a small phylum of about 90 species, somewhat similar to coelenterates but possessing several unique features. The most conspicuous of these is eight rows of paddle-like structures composed of heavy cilia by which the animal paddles its way, mouth foremost, through the water; another is the curious internal structure of canals underlying the rows of combs, which are in turn connected with the central gut. The comb jellies are hermaphroditic, with the ovaries and testes arranged on each side of the canals. All

[55]

ctenophores have a pair of tentacles in their young stage, but one group loses them as adults. They lack nematocysts, and their sexual arrangement is distinct from jellyfish.

Swimming ctenophores are easily recognized, if placed in a jar of sea water, by the irridescent sparkling of the combs. Although not intertidal animals, they are sometimes common in the bays and near shore. The Sea Gooseberry, or Sea Walnut, *Pleurobrachia bachei*, looks somewhat like the diagram; it is nearly spherical and about the size of a finger tip. Large, flat ctenophores without tentacles are species of *Beroë*.

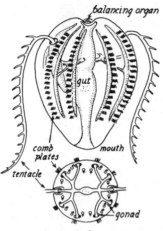

A ctenophore:
Cross-section showing canals and gonads.

PLATYHELMINTHES: Flatworms

The flatworms include the tapeworms, flukes, and the free-living Turbellaria. These are leaf-like creatures that slip over the surface of a rock so closely that it is almost impossible to remove them intact with a fingernail. Such flatworms are carnivorous and prey upon barnacles, bryozoans, young oysters, and clams. Some flatworms are spectacular, striped or mottled animals, but our common species of the genus *Leptoplana* are rather drab, light brown worms. The more brightly colored ones are not rare in the Monterey area and are sometimes found swimming in the tide pools on a good early tide. Those striped white and black are probably species of *Pseudoceros*. Identification of these animals requires microscopic examination of the reproductive system from thin slices (sections) prepared according to procedures somewhat reminiscent of alchemy.

NEMERTEA: Ribbon Worms

Ribbon worms are considered to be related to flatworms and do resemble them in having no internal cavity, but they have several distinct features, the most noteworthy of which is the proboscis. This is an elaborate, eversible structure, carried in a space above the digestive tract, that works like a glove finger by turning inside out, and is retracted by a slender muscle. The proboscis is used in capturing prey, often comparatively large worms, by wrapping around the body of the victim. In some species the tip is armed with spines or stylets. The digestive tract is long, unbranched, and with a terminal anus. There is also a circulatory system, consisting mostly of longitudinal vessels. The body wall is lined with circular and longitudinal muscles, and nemerteans move by producing forward-moving muscular waves along the body. Sexes are separate.

An old theory, recently revived, postulates the nemerteans as being in the chordate line, because there are structures resembling gill slits and because the proboscis occurs in the position of the notochord. In any event, nemerteans are not very much like flatworms except in their carnivorous habit.

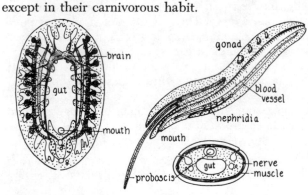

Schematic anatomy of a flatworm (left) and a nemertean (right)

Of the 750 or more species known, at least 31 are found along the central California coast. Some are brightly colored, solid red or orange; others are striped, banded, or spotted. Most are marine and free living, but one terrestrial species, *Geonemertes,* is common under boards and stones on the marshes, and several of the genus *Malocobdella* occur in clams.

There are two common species at higher tide levels. The greenish, slender ribbon worm with whitish lower surface is *Emplectonema gracile,* found in the mussel beds. A somewhat thicker, brownish or purplish worm, often in the same situation, is *Paranemertes peregrina.* Both of these may be several inches long but are capable of changing their length, and the old question about the length of a piece of string is even less answerable for these animals. They most closely resemble sticky bootlaces strung about the mussels.

ANNELIDA: Segmented Worms

The annelid worms include the familiar Earthworm, the leeches, and several thousand species of marine worms bearing bristles, or chaetae, in bundles on most segments. The annelids have a coelom, nephridia, and reproductive organs repeated in each segment behind the head (with, of course, the usual exceptions), and the marine species develop by spiral cleavage and have a trochophore larva. The repetition of similar segments is called metamerism. In some groups of worms the metameres, or somites, are specialized in regions that resemble in a beginning way the well-defined differentiation (tagmosis) of the arthropods. In many basic features, worms and arthropods are difficult to separate, and some zoologists consider them one large phylum, Articulata or Annulata. In Plate 6 we have indicated these relationships by a hypothetical, generalized ancestral type, the Lobopod. In their embryonic beginnings, annelids are almost indistinguishable from mol-

[58]

luscs, and the discovery of the deep sea limpet, *Neopilina*, with its repeated kidneys and gonads, is further confirmation of this relationship. In the distant past there seems to have been a divergence from an even lower common denominator than the Lobopod, giving rise on one hand to a segmented stock culminating in the arthropods and, on the other hand, to an unsegmented stock (with some repetition of organs) that led to modern molluscs.

Related in some way or another to annelids, but lacking segmentation and in other respects distinct enough to merit separate phyletic rank, are the echiurid and sipunculid worms. They evidently represent separate specializations in another direction. However, in a book or list things must be arranged one after the other, often without respect to natural order. Hence, the reader will find the echiurids and sipunculids between the annelids and the arthropods, simply because three-dimensional printing is not practical.

POLYCHAETES: Bristle Worms

The polychaetes are marine worms almost exclusively. Although they have the same basic features of the earthworm, they differ in being armed with bunches of bristles (hence the name Polychaeta) mounted on lateral lobes or parapodia. Many of them are armed with formidable biting jaws and groups of tentacles on the head. Others are apparently headless and lack jaws but have elaborate branched bills or plumelike feeding structures. In fact, there is such a fantastic diversity among marine "bristle worms" (some of which have almost no bristles at all) that classification is difficult. No clear-cut, major divisions are discernible among polychaetes, and the two broad divisions are essentially based on habit, so we recognize the wandering or errant worms and the sedentary worms.

Among the errant worms the most commonly seen are

nereids, often used as bait; the most common of these is *Nereis vexillosa,* an iridescent green or brownish worm, found under stones, among mussels, and on piling. On bay shores a similar worm, *Neanthes succinea,* may be abundant. At times of sexual activity these worms take on a somewhat different structure and swim

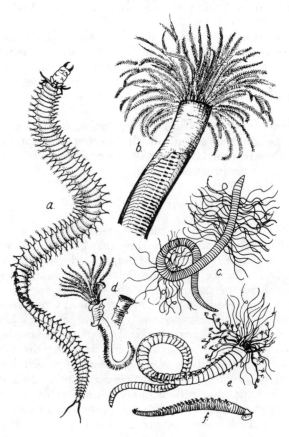

a: *Nereis vexillosa* (× 1); b: *Eudistylia polymorpha* (× 1); c: *Cirriformia* (× 1/2); d: *Mercierella enigmata* (with end of tube) (× 2); e: *Pista pacifica* (× 1/2); f: *Pectinophelia dillonensis* (× 1).

actively in the water with a rapid sinuous motion; these heteronereis stages of *Neanthes* are sometimes abundant in San Francisco Bay. Both of these worms may be several inches long and have over a hundred segments. It may be the luck of a beginner to encounter an enormous green worm several feet long: the serpent-like proportions of *Nereis brandti* may unnerve the amateur, but the worm is harmless.

Still another nereid, *Nereis diversicolor* (or *Nereis lighti*), is to be found on bay shores, especially in areas of reduced salinity, and some races of this worm will withstand water that is almost completely fresh. Along the California coast, at places like the mouth of the Salinas River and the estuaries of small creeks, there are populations of this worm that are self-fertilizing, viviparous hermaphrodites. If one defines a species as an interbreeding population, as some systematists do, each individual worm is virtually a species by itself.

The digger in sandy beaches may find brilliant red worms of the family Opheliidae, an inch or two long, about 18 inches below the surface. Like most polychaetes this is a brilliantly iridescent animal, and many people who are at first repelled by the thought of studying worms become fascinated by the beauty and variety of polychaetes, The Red Beachworm is a member of a group which seems very particular about the kind of place it lives in, and the larvae of related European species have demonstrated preferences for particular kinds of sand. Our species at Dillon Beach is *Pectinophelia dillonensis*, and lives only in fine, clean beach sand.

Sedentary polychaetes include many kinds of tube builders. The snow-white calcareous tubes found on the under surfaces of rocks are made by *Serpula*, which has a bright red crown of tentacles that may be withdrawn in the proverbial flash. In the bays a related worm forms dense, dingy gray tube masses; this worm, *Mercierella enigmata*, is especially common in Lake

[61]

Merritt but is found in many parts of the world in both northern and southern hemispheres. Other types of tube worms build parchment-like tubes in crevices or among the mussels on piling. The most conspicuous of these is *Eudistyla polymorpha,* whose "feather duster" of tentacles is conspicuously purple, reddish, tan, or sometimes banded. On sandy mud flats a curious gray tube with a ragged flap over the top is common. Anyone who tries to dig this up will find that the tube is at least two feet long, and that it is inhabited by a worm with an elaborately branched set of gills at the head end and bright, red blood conspicuous in the large vessels. This is *Pista pacifica.* In the puddles left on the flats the orange filaments of *Cirriformia* are conspicuous.

There is almost no end to the variety of polychaetes occurring in the varied habitats of the seashore, but identification requires study of the bristles, or setae, and of processes about the head that are not easily seen. Perhaps these difficulties explain the lack of any comprehensive manual for polychaetes, despite their beauty and importance in the economy of the sea.

ECHIURIDA

Echiurid worms are very abundant in some places. On the shallow bottoms south of Santa Barbara one species, *Listriolobus pelodes,* occurs by the millions over many square miles. However, only one species is common along the shore, as indicated in the synopsis. This is *Urechis caupo,* the Fat Innkeeper or Weenie Worm. It lives in a permanent ∪-shaped burrow, which is also inhabited by some associates (commensals) who live on the crumbs from its table. These include a small fish, a scale worm, and a small clam. Most echiurids feed by means of elaborate proboscides which gather detritus from the surface or fall upon them through the water; they are often called "spoon worms." *Urechis,* however, is an atypical echiurid. Its proboscis is reduced

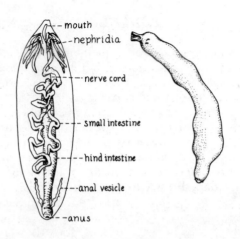

Echiurid anatomy   *Urechis caupo* ($\times$ 1/5)

to a lip, and it produces a fine-meshed funnel of mucus with which it strains small particles from the water it pumps through its burrow by peristalsis of its flexibile body. The sexes in *Urechis* are separate; in some echiurids the large worm is a female, and the male is a minute vestigial sort of creature that lives as a parasite in the nephridium of its mate. In such species the very young worm can become either sex: if it settles on or near a female, it migrates inside and develops only into a male. In this case the male is essentially an arrested female. *Urechis* has hemoglobin in corpuscles loose in its coelom.

Collecting Weenie Worms is quite a chore. First the holes must be identified, usually by inserting a rubber tube and blowing to locate the other end. The tube is then poked in as far as possible as a guide to the digger, who must then excavate a trench about three feet deep. Often the trench caves in before the worm is found, and the process must be started all over again with a new victim. A large *Urechis* (a foot long or more) may be several decades old.

Sipunculids are characteristically inhabitants of crevices and crannies ("nestlers"), but some of them occur under rocks, with their lower bodies in sulfide mud. This is possible for them because their anus is not posterior but located up toward the front end of the animal. There are several common species, but identification is often a matter of dissection. The commonest species is *Phascolosoma agassizi* (illustrated in the synopsis), a brownish-bodied peanut worm, up to about 2 inches long, with dark brown to purplish irregular spots. It may be found in the mussel beds and among the roots of surf grass. Lower down, *Dendrostomum pyroides* is a common species. A large burrowing form, *Sipunculus nudus,* silvery white with a rectangular network of fine grooves, is occasionally encountered. It may be 6–8 inches long. A number of sipunculids rejoice in the "scientific" generic name of *Golfingia,* so named in honor of an afternoon on the golf links by an eminent pillar of Victorian zoology, Sir E. Ray Lankester. Many sipunculids have a peculiar purplish blood pigment, hemerythrin.

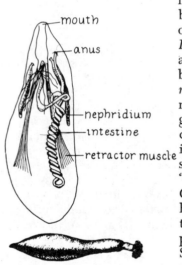

Sipunculid anatomy;
Dendrostoma pyroides (× 1/2).

ARTHROPODA

The arthropods, or jointed-legged ones, constitute the largest group of animals. Perhaps a million species

[64]

Outer, wave-swept coast
(Pebble Beach, Pescadero)

Semiprotected coast
(Dillon Beach)

Zonation, middle zones

Zonation at low tide, showing
ascidians, sponges, bryozoa

Left:
Surf grass

Right:
Sandy beach

PLATE 1

Hermissenda crassicornis,
Phyllaplysia zostericola

Anthopleura xanthogrammica,
Strongylocentrotus purpuratus

Rhabdodermella nuttingi

Hermissenda crassicornis

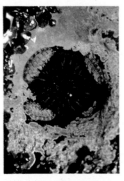

Strongylocentrotus franciscanus,
Tonicella lineata, Lithothamnion

Pollicipes polymerus

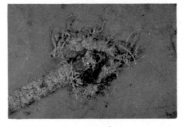

Pista pacifica

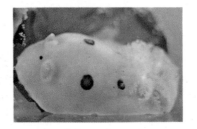

Diaulula sandiegensis

PLATE 2

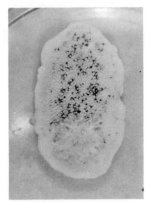

Anisodoris nobilis

Pycnogonids and caprellid
on *Aglaophenia*

Triopha maculata

Pachygrapsus crassipes

Sea lions and sea elephants

PLATE 3

PLATE 4. Sea stars (painting by Norman Mayer)
Pisaster ochraceous (×1/5) *Pisaster brevispinus* (×1/5)
Henricia leviuscula (×2/5) *Pycnopodia helianthoides* (×1/10)
Leptasterias aequalis (×2/5) *Patiria miniata* (×3/10)
Dermasterias imbricata (×1/3)

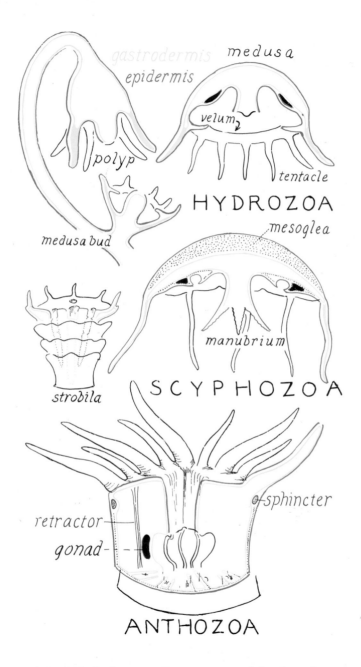

PLATE 5. Coelenterata. Basic structure of the three classes.

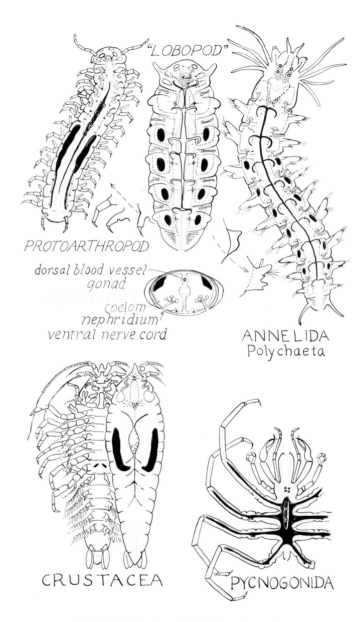

"LOBOPOD"

PROTOARTHROPOD

dorsal blood vessel
gonad

coelom
nephridium
ventral nerve cord

ANNELIDA
Polychaeta

CRUSTACEA

PYCNOGONIDA

PLATE 6. The Annelid-Arthropod complex.
Basic structure of Crustacea and Pycnogonida,
characteristically marine arthropods.

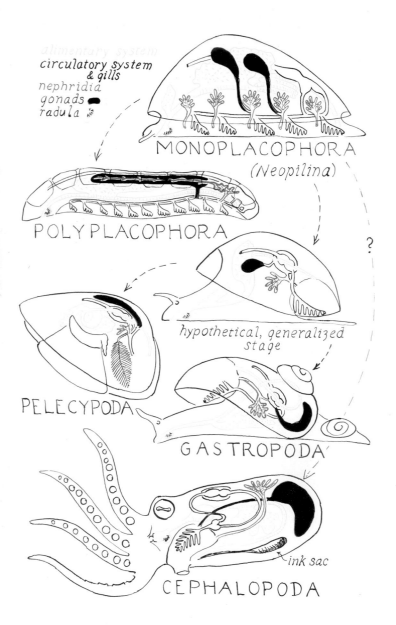

PLATE 7. Mollusca.
The major classes and their inferred evolution.

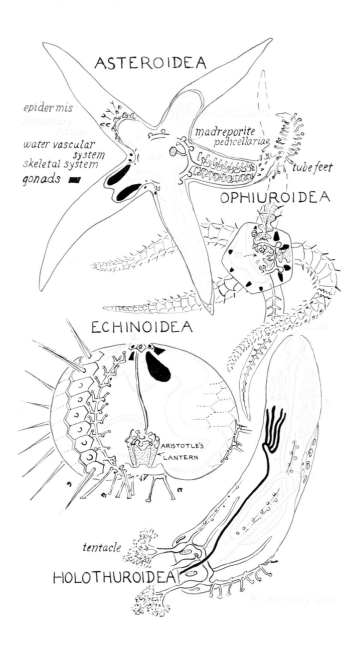

ASTEROIDEA

epidermis

alimentary system

water vascular system

skeletal system

gonads

madreporite

pedicellariae

tube feet

OPHIUROIDEA

ECHINOIDEA

ARISTOTLE'S LANTERN

tentacle

HOLOTHUROIDEA

PLATE 8. Echinoderma. Basic schemes of the four classes represented on the shore (Crinoidea omitted).

are known, of which more than three-fourths are insects. Crustaceans, the characteristic arthropods of the sea, including the copepods, barnacles, shrimps, crabs, and lesser legions, are twenty-five or thirty thousand strong. If we set aside the possession of wings by many insects, the range of variation is comparatively small in such basic matters as numbers of appendages and body segments as compared with the crustacea. Insects are characteristically air breathers, and this dependence on atmospheric air may explain their rarity in the ocean (a few beetles and flies live along the shore). Another large terrestrial group, the Arachnids, consisting of spiders, scorpions, ticks, and mites, are almost as unsuccessful in the sea as insects, except for a number of marine mites. One group of arthropods, not clearly related to any terrestrial or fresh water group is the Pycnogonida, or sea spiders. There are some 500 species of these, and several of them are common along the shore among hydroids and on sea anemones.

Although the arthropods are clearly related to the annelid worms in their basic structure, their coelom has been reduced to the collecting sac of the excretory organs, and these organs are reduced in Crustacea to one or two pairs, and replaced in the insects by the Malpighian tubules, which are associated with the hindgut. Instead of the large coelom of the annelid, the body cavity of the arthropod is essentially the expanded venous system, or hemocoel. No arthropod hatches as a primitive, trochophore-like larva. The youngest larval stage is the nauplius, which is the usual larval stage of the copepods, water fleas, fairy shrimps, barnacles, and some shrimps. Most shrimps and crabs have a somewhat more advanced larval stage, the zooea, and one large group, which includes the pill bugs and beach hoppers, possess a brood pouch in which the eggs are hatched as miniatures not greatly different from their parents. (This type of development is termed "direct.")

Evolution of the arthropods is principally evident in

the manner of specialization of the various body regions. This process reaches its highest specialization in the insects, where the total number of segments has been reduced to form easily recognized head, thorax, and abdomen. In the pycnogonids, which seem to be relatively unspecialized, the head is part of the first group of segments that include the first pair of legs, but the abdomen is reduced to little more than a process for the anus. Various grades of specialization are exemplified by the Crustacea, beginning with the fairy shrimp, which have a well-developed head, but do not have a clearly separable thorax or abdomen, and culminating in the crabs, which are essentially head and thorax in one compact unit with a flap-like abdomen curled underneath.

Because of their great variety and range of structure, Crustacea are not easily defined in simple terms. All of them at one stage or another possess branched, second antennae (the long, whip-like feelers so conspicuous on lobsters and crayfish), and the larger ones bear breathing structures or gills on or near the legs (except the air-breathing pill bugs and the many crustaceans such as copepods, which are small enough to get along without a breathing system). The characters of a fairly advanced crustacean are represented in Plate 7, along with those of a pycnogonid. The latter creatures are somewhat simpler; they have no antennae, and consist mostly of legs. The digestive tract and reproductive system have long branches reaching into the legs, and there is no special breathing system.

PYCNOGONIDA

Sea spiders are sometimes abundant, and one may be conspicuous as a salmon pink or whitish creature, perhaps half an inch long, at the base of a large green sea anemone. This is *Pycnogonum stearnsi*. A much smaller but conspicuously green pycnogonid is often abundant

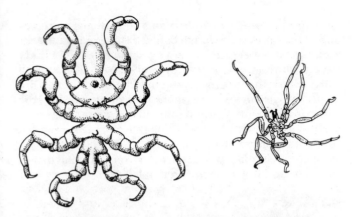

Pycnogonum stearnsi ($\times$ 4)　　*Halosoma viridintestinale* ($\times$ 8)

on the *Obelia* attached to eel-grass in sheltered waters. This is *Halosoma viridintenstinale*: young stages develop in *Obelia,* forming swellings in the hydranths. There are a dozen or so other species that may be seen by anyone who decides to inspect hydroids and other growth under a hand lens. Often pycnogonids will be seen carrying small bundles or clusters of eggs on their lower surfaces; these are the males. The females are larger, and in some genera, *Pycnogonum,* for example, they lack the extra pair of small legs that the male uses to hold the eggs.

CRUSTACEA

COPEPODA

Copepods are legion in the sea and are among the most numerous and important members of the zooplankton. Upon their well-being depends in turn the prosperity of populations of fishes. Some of these oceanic copepods are a quarter of an inch or more long, but the shore species are small and inconspicuous. Most of these encountered are not active swimmers but crawlers and grovellers on the surfaces of plants and attached animals and in the loose sand and detritus of the crevices among rocks. Most copepods (except those that may be blind) have a conspicuous single eye, often red like a small ruby under the microscope. One species is often observed by anyone who happens to peer closely into the little pools of water caught high on the rocks. This copepod, which looks like specks of red pepper swimming in pools no larger than a cup of water, is *Tigriopus californicus*. It is a hardy animal, easily kept in small dishes of water, and it is now cultured in laboratories.

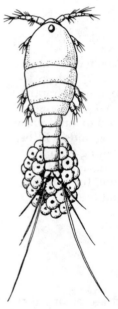
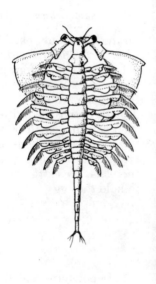

Tigriopus californicus (× 35)   *Artemia salina* (× 5)

PHYLLOPODA: Fairy shrimps

Fairy shrimps are more characteristically creatures of the temporary pools of springtime, but one species is famous for the great ranges of salt concentration in

[76]

which it can thrive. This is the brine shrimp, *Artemia salina,* a conspicuous inhabitant of the ponds in which sea water is evaporated for its salt in the southern part of San Francisco Bay. The eggs of *Artemia* are viable for years and may be hatched without too much difficulty, even in nearly fresh water. They are available commercially as food for tropical fishes, and as they hatch as nauplii, the eggs provide the best source of material for observation of this larval type.

Barnacles start out as honest crustaceans with a nauplius larva. This changes into a bivalved larva, the cypris, which in turn settles on its head and develops into the barnacle. The barnacle is attached by the back of its neck, loses most of its head, and lives thereafter by kicking food into its mouth. Some barnacles grow little volcano-like shells formed of plates; others develop a fleshy stalk and carry the plates like armor covering their body. Other barnacles become parasites and live like lumpy cancers on crabs.

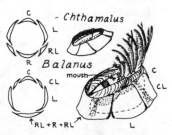

Barnacle genera

The most noticeable of our common shore barnacles is the white Acorn Barnacle, *Balanus glandula,* found high up on rocks and piling everywhere along the ocean shore and in the saltier regions of San Francisco Bay. In San Pablo Bay, in less saline water, it is replaced by *Balanus improvisus.* Lower down on the rocks of the ocean shore is the larger Thatched Barnacle, *Balanus cariosus.* A smaller, often brownish and somewhat flatter barnacle occupies the highest position of barnacles on our shores, but it is mingled with

[77]

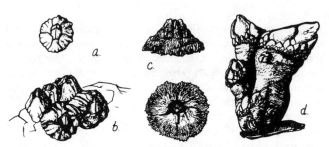

a: *Chthamalus dalli* (× 2); b: *Balanus glandula* (× 1); c: *Balanus cariosus* (× 1); d: *Pocillipes polymerus* (× 1).

Balanus glandula. This is *Chthamalus dalli.* The differences between *Balanus* and *Chthamalus* are best understood by inspecting the diagram.

Our common Stalked or Leaf Barnacle is *Pollicipes polymerus,* (formerly *Mitella*). It forms dense clusters and bands about mid-tide level on rocky shores from Canada to Mexico, and together with the California Mussel and the Ochre Star it makes up the most characteristic association of marine animals on our coast. Barnacles are usually considered to be rather dainty feeders, sieving fine things out of the water with their feather-like feet, but the Leaf Barnacle captures fairly large food, dead or alive, that comes its way. Barnacles have poor eyes, and are usually active only when submerged or at least damp, but Leaf Barnacles are sensitive to shadows and will move slowly when a hand is passed over a cluster that has been in the sunlight when the tide is out.

Although not a shore dweller, the Goose Barnacle, *Lepas anatifera,* is often seen attached to logs and other flotsam cast ashore. It has a long, rubbery brown stalk and bluish white plates with bright orange trimmings.

LESSER CRUSTACEANS

Among the numerous types of crustaceans that are either inconspicuous or not easily identified by the amateur, the ostracods are the least noticeable because of their small size. These are small, pod-shaped creatures with two valves, sometimes common in the warm sloughs of the bay shores and among the detritus of the ocean shore. In structure they are like the cypris larva of barnacles. They are mostly about a millimeter or so in length. Often a fairly conspicuous, white, flea-like animal with a long "tail" is seen in the green scummy or stringy algae of bay flats, skittering about on its side. This creature is a nebaliid of the genus *Epinebalia*.

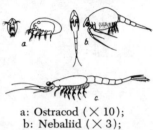

a: Ostracod ($\times$ 10);
b: Nebaliid ($\times$ 3);
c: Mysid ($\times$ 1).

Like an ostracod, it has two valves, but it has other features that identify it with the higher crustacea such as shrimps and crabs. In the surf and swash pools on sandy beaches and in brackish waters, mysids are often abundant. These are transparent shrimp-like animals about an inch long, distantly related to beach-hoppers and the like because the females brood their eggs in a pouch. For this reason mysids are also called Opossum shrimps.

ISOPODA

Isopods are often numerous, and several of them are common. They are so named because their legs are of about equal length and appearance. Their bodies are flattened like badgers. The familiar sow- or pill-bug is an isopod, and a few marine isopods such as *Alloniscus*, high up on sandy beaches, can roll up in a similar manner, but most of our shore species cannot do this.

The most easily observed isopod is the Rock Louse, *Ligia occidentalis*, which stays above the tide and can be seen, especially at dusk or on cloudy days, scurrying over rocks and into crevices. In this region its range overlaps with that of its much larger northern cousin,

[79]

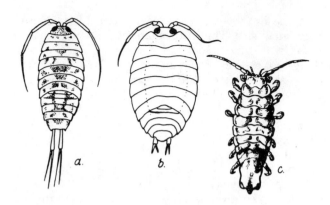

a: *Ligia occidentalis* (× 1); b: *Ligia pallasi* (× 1); c: *Idothea stenops* (× 1/2).

Ligia pallasi. Among seaweeds and in sheltered places at lower levels there are some very large (up to 2 inches long) sluggish isopods of the genus *Idothea*. There are several species of these, not easily identified except by experts. The Rock Louse is an omnivorous scavenger which thrives well on picnic leavings, while *Idothea* is a seaweed eater. One isopod is a wood eater and often causes damage to piling, which it chews into an hourglass shape at mid-tide level. This is the Gribble, *Limnoria*, which can be seen as a pale, grub-like creature about a tenth of an inch long in bits of wood broken off from infected piling.

AMPHIPODA

Amphipods differ from isopods in having longer legs at both ends, and in being flattened from side to side instead of from top to bottom. If a visitor to the shore walks down a sandy beach in the evening or early morning, the large beach-hoppers of the genus *Orchestoidea* may be the first living invertebrate he sees (there is always a bird or two in every seascape). Beach-hoppers

Orchestoidea ($\times$ 2): left, *O. californiana*; right, *O. corniculata*. Drawing by Darl Bowers.

can often be found under the rotting seaweed at the crest of the beach, and during the daytime the larger ones conceal themselves in burrows several inches below the surface of the sand. The antics of the larger ones will provide hours of entertainment for those who go to the beach at night with a flashlight. Smaller beach-hoppers are members of the genus *Orchestia*, but all amphipods are difficult to identify. They are all active scavengers and do their best to keep the beach clean, although they have not learned to eat cans, bottles, and plastic containers.

If clumps of the bushier seaweeds are placed in a pan of water, flea-like animals will swim out. These are also amphipods, of such genera as *Melita* and *Anisogammarus*.

A somewhat different amphipod is the Skeleton Shrimp, *Caprella*, often abundant on hydroids. It is attached by its hind legs and bows back and forth at passing objects.

DECAPODA

The most advanced (in some respects) crustaceans belong to the order Decapoda, meaning that they have ten walking or swimming legs. This count includes the claws of crabs, but not the feelers or antennae nor the often very large last pair of mouth parts (maxillipeds) The shrimps and crabs present a bewildering gradation of structural patterns that sometimes makes their classification difficult. We will divide them into Macrura, the big-tailed shrimps and lobsters, the Anomura, the somewhat intermediate crustaceans that include hermit crabs, burrowing shrimp, and others, and the short-tailed Brachyura, the "true" crabs. Even specialists do not always agree as to just how to divide these three groups. In general, a crab-like animal with the eyes between the antennae is an anomuran, and the reverse arrangement is that of a brachyuran.

a: Grass shrimp, *Hippolyte;* b: Broken back shrimp, *Spironto-caris,* showing comparative segments of the second leg.

Macrura

Anyone who fishes with a dip net in a tide pool or shakes out some large bushy seaweeds into a pan will find several shrimp between one and two inches long. Most of these will have a broken-backed appearance and come in various shades of brown, pink, and green. These are *Spirontocaris,* of which there is a bewildering variety of species. A slenderer, green shrimp without such a conspicuous kink in the back, usually found on eel grass, is *Hippolyte californica.* The difference between these two genera is in the number of segments on the second leg, which will appear to be the third leg because of the large maxilliped. Gray shrimp, 2-3 inches long, in large swash pools along the sandy beach or in large tide pools, are members of the genus *Crago.* The common species, *Crago franciscorum,* is uniform gray, without a big black spot on the tail (*C. nigrocauda*), or on the side of the abdomen just before the tail (*C. nigromaculata*). In recent years a new shrimp has

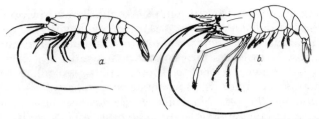

a: *Crago franciscorum;* b: *Palaemon macrodactylus* (both ×1/2).

appeared in San Francisco Bay and may in time replace *Crago franciscorum.* It is about 2 inches long and will live in brackish water; since 1957, when it was first noticed in the Bay, it has moved upstream past Collins-ville and Antioch. This is *Palaemon macrodactylus,* in-troduced from the Orient in some inadvertent manner, perhaps in sea-water tanks from returning ships.

Anomura

Among the shrimp-like anomurans are two burrowing or ghost shrimps which, although common, are not often seen except by those who dig industriously in the bay flats. The villages of the large pink Ghost Shrimp, *Cal-lianassa californiensis,* occur about mid-tide level in sandier areas, and are easily identified because the openings to the burrows are raised on low conical hills. The lining of the burrows is smooth and firmer than the surrounding sand, and the diameter is "choked" toward the top. The shrimp itself, which feeds by filtering small

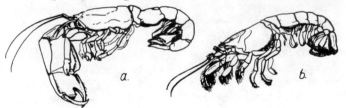

a: *Callianassa californiensis;* b: *Upogebia pugettensis* (both × 1/3).

fry out of the water it pumps through its burrow, may be nearly six inches long, and it can pinch with its large claws. Usually the excavation caves in long before the animal is reached, but sometimes a stealthy approach, with a quick stroke of the shovel a foot or so below the top of the burrow, produces successful results (or a bisected shrimp). Sometimes *Callianassa* is found outside its burrow, helplessly vulnerable and possibly *in extremis*. Lower down on the flats, in muddier bottoms, will be found the related Mud Shrimp, *Upogebia pugettensis*. It is stockier and smaller than *Callianassa* and has a flattened, triangular, hardened area with short spines between the eyes. Its color is bluish.

Hermit crabs are of course abundant in the tide pools, and at low tide some of them hide between clusters of aggregated anemones and similar shelter. The abdomen is modified to slip into a snail shell. Hermit crabs are among the favorite objects of seashore observers, and their antics are discussed in detail in almost every account of seashore life. Our common species all belong to the genus *Pagurus*. If the antennae are the same color as the body, the species is probably *Pagurus hirsutiusculus*. If it has red antennae and blue or white bands

Pagurus, a hermit crab ($\times$ 1)

Emerita analoga ($\times$ 2/3)

[84]

on the legs, it is probably *Pagurus samuelis*. Beyond this, things get more complicated and anyhow, everybody knows what a hermit crab is.

On sandy beaches, tumbled about by moving waves, the egg-shaped Sand Crabs, *Emerita analoga*, are often conspicuous. The large females may be about one and a half inches long—the size of a young pullet's first effort—and usually carry clusters of bright orange eggs beneath the reflexed tail. If the eggs are darker orange, they are nearer hatching. The males are smaller and often live somewhat higher up on the beach. These animals dig best in sand of a certain moisture content, and it is probably the amount of water in the sand, rather than the actual height of the tide, that governs their position on the beach. Like many animals, they have good and bad years. Sometimes they occur by the millions; other times only a few may be found along the open sandy beach.

Under rocks there are two—of several—flattened crabs, with somewhat triangular claws or chelipeds, that scuttle actively away as the rock is lifted. *Petrolisthes cinctipes,* the Flat or Porcelain Crab, is the most abundant and lively of these. Another, living in deeper crevices and somewhat less active, has much heavier claws. This is *Pachycheles rudis.* If pursued too strenuously,

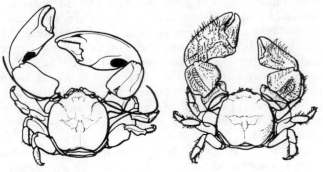

Petrolisthes cinctipes ($\times$ 1)   *Pachycheles rudis* ($\times$ 1)

[85]

these crabs will willingly shed a claw in the cause of freedom. There are several species of both genera. These crabs are the most brachyuran of the anomuran crabs, but their larval stages are strikingly different, bearing long spear-like processes fore and aft, whereas brachyuran zooea are more rounded and resemble ancient helmets.

Brachyura: Crabs

The common, characteristic crab of rocky shores is the Lined Shore Crab, *Pachygrapsus crassipes*, often seen lurking in damp crevices. The carapace is greenish, with reddish or purplish transverse stripes, and the large claws are reddish on the upper surface. It is about 2 inches wide. This is an active crab, best caught unawares by turning a loose rock near high-tide level. In the open, giving a fair start, it is elusive and difficult to catch. While there is some question among the experts as to whether a crab really has a brain capable of premeditated thought, many frustrated beachcombers are of the opinion that the crab's power of thought is not open to question.

A somewhat similar crab, without the transverse markings and with reddish purple spots on the claws, lives somewhat lower down the shore and is less active; this is *Hemigrapsus nudus*. On bay shores, especially in muddy banks and under stones, will be found the dull greenish *Hemigrapsus oregonensis*. Several larger crabs are occasionally found, especially half-imbedded in sand near large rocks or in tide pools. These large crabs belong to the genus *Cancer* and include the commercial crab (*Cancer magister*), which is not a shore species. The usual species among rocks is *Cancer antennarius*.

One of the common crabs of seaweed growths is a slow-moving, somewhat angular crab with small claws (which nevertheless has a strong bite), whose color so

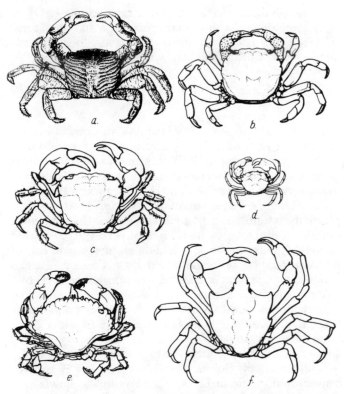

a: *Pachygrapsus crassipes* (× 1/2); b: *Hemigrapsus nudus* (× 1/2); c: *Hemigrapsus oregonensis* (× 1/2); d: *Rithropanopeus harrisi* (× 1/2); e: *Cancer antennarius* (× 1/5); f: *Pugettia producta* (× 1/2).

much resembles the brown seaweed that it may be overlooked or inadvertently picked up. This is the Kelp crab, *Pugettia producta.*

At some time or another, at least twenty years ago, a small crab about three-fourths of an inch wide, from the Atlantic coast, dull-greenish with whitish under-surface, established itself in San Francisco Bay and is now common in sloughs as far up as Napa and Stockton. This is *Rithropanopeus harrisi.* It has also been found in the sloughs near Coos Bay, Oregon.

MOLLUSCA
(Plate 7)

In the arthropods we have many variations in external form and arrangements of appendages to correspond with the varied ways of life of this most numerous group of animals. Their internal anatomy, however, is not as greatly varied as that of their kindred group, the molluscs. Here we have variations in internal structure, plasticity within a lump of viscera, rather than permutations of appendages. This visceral versatility reaches its highest point in the squids and octopuses, with complete circulation of blood aided by accessory hearts, and nervous system surpassed in complexity only by that of man and porpoise.

Both molluscs and arthropods are "blue-blooded" animals; their blood contains as its active respiratory element a complex molecule containing an atom of copper, instead of the ring of atoms with iron at its center that is found in hemoglobin. This blue pigment is called hemocyanin. Some arthropods and molluscs, however, possess red blood, and no evolutionary significance can be attached to the type of blood pigment an animal possesses. The circulatory systems of both phyla are open; that is, there is no well-developed venous system, but instead, a series of spaces or sinuses. The heart is near the upper side in a sac called the pericardium, with a few long simple arteries leading from it.

Until the discovery of the deep sea limpet, *Neopilina,* off the coast of Central America a few years ago, there were considered to be five principal living classes of molluscs. *Neopilina* is a living representative of a Paleozoic class, the Monoplacophora, so now we must consider six classes as living. Only four classes, however,

[88]

are commonly found on the sea shore. There are the Amphineura or Polyplacophora—the chitons; the Gastropoda, or snails and slugs; the Pelecypoda, or bivalves; and the Cephalopods. On the central California coast the chitons, whose internal structure resembles the Monoplacophora, at least in nervous system and perhaps muscles, are represented out of all proportion to their numbers, while gastropods are perhaps not quite as numerous in species as they might be. Bivalves are quite well represented, but usually only a single cephalopod, a small octopus of uncertain identity, is found.

The remaining class is the Scaphopoda, or tooth shells, a comparatively small group of sand and mud-burrowing molluscs with a cylindrical, curved, and tapered shell open at both ends. These animals have numerous filament-like tentacles at the head end (which is downward in the mud) and feed on such things as foraminifera and other small prey. Some get very large, and the shells are occasionally available as curios in such places as the Nut Tree restaurant. Except for their curvature, they could be used as cigarette holders.

We can derive a chiton from a segmented limpet (*Neopilina*) by reduction of repeated internal organs and division of the elongated shell into manageable dimensions by separate plates (which bear no relation to original segments.) The gastropod is more complex. As the animal grew in size, the shell became taller and less manageable, and the spiral was discovered, lowering the center of gravity. Before or after, the numbers of repeated internal organs were reduced. Somewhere in their history the gastropods learned a useful trick called torsion. By this 180-degree rotation within the shell, the snail has managed to pack itself more snugly into its shell. Many snails, however, have subsequently become straightened out, although in the course of their embryology they still go through some of the motions of torsion. Many such snails have lost their shells and are now sea slugs.

The bivalves represent still another direction of modification—overgrowth of the shell and subsequent division of it in two halves, held together by a strong adductor muscle. With this modification has come the loss of head and much of the nervous system. Variation among clams and mussels is expressed in the complex arrangements of the gills, which are the principal feeding structures of these animals. That most characteristic of molluscan structures, the radula or narrow ribbon of teeth that functions like a sanding machine, is absent from the bivalves.

The radula is present in the cephalopods, together with a strong tearing beak. Most modern cephalopods have lost the shell, which was once the crowning glory of this class of molluscs, if we are to judge from the fossil evidence; they are soft-bodied, mobile animals with well-developed eyes, whose structure is very much like that of vertebrates, and the foot and head region is modified into eight tentacles with unstalked suckers in the octopus. Squids have ten tentacles, and the suckers have short stalks. Apparently the radula is of some use to an octopus, as it may drill small holes in limpets and abalones, through which it can then inject toxic fluids to induce the prey to give up its hold on the rock—and life.

Amphineura: Chitons

Chitons are especially abundant, both in numbers and species, on this coast. In the Monterey area some 29 species have been found along the shore, and there are many other deeper water species that may stray upwards. Chitons are usually considered herbivorous, grazing on seaweeds and diatoms, but several are at least half carnivorous in habit, feeding on Bryozoa, barnacles, and small mussels. Positive identification of these molluscs often requires taking them apart and counting the teeth or notches on the plates, and the identity of many species is not certain even to experts, because of the changes with age, variations in color, and alterations of the plates by erosion. Therefore we can offer only a sampling of some of the common species.

Chitons are best prepared for study by strapping them gently but firmly to a flat stick as soon as they are collected. They are then killed by placing them in warm, fresh water or directly in preservative. All molluscs should be preserved in alcohol, as formalin will attack the shell.

The Gum Boot, *Cryptochiton stelleri,* is easy to identify because of its large size (up to a foot long) and the orange-brown covering that completely conceals the

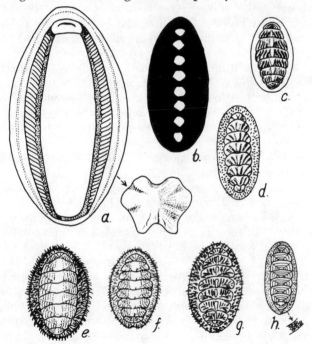

a: *Cryptochiton stelleri* (and a valve) (× 1/5); b: *Katherina tunicata* (× 1/2); c: *Tonicella lineata* (× 2/3); d: *Nuttalina californica* (× 2/3); e: *Mopalia muscosa* (× 2/3); f: *M. ciliata* (× 2/3); g: *M. lignosa* (× 2/3); h: *Ischnochiton regularis* (× 2/3).

valves. The separated valves or plates, often found on the beach, cause some puzzlement; they are often called "butterfly shells." Cryptochitons occur fairly low down and are more abundant further north. They make poor specimens and cannot be eaten, as the foot is extraordinarly tough and the mantle is so full of spicules that eating this equally tough portion would be about as good for the teeth as a sandpaper salad. Yet valves of *Cryptochiton* are common in Indian mounds; perhaps the Indians ate only the guts and gonads.

Another chiton easy to recognize is the Black Chiton, *Katharina tunicata*. It has a shiny black mantle almost covering the valves, which show as separated white structures. The Black Chiton may reach a length of almost five inches and often occurs well above mid-tide level.

The highest chiton, in terms of residence, is *Nuttallina californica*. This is a dingy, greenish-gray chiton with short bristles on the region around the valves (the girdle). The valves are brownish and have V-shaped ridges, which are often worn down showing white markings. *Nuttallina* is usually the first chiton encountered by visitors to a rocky shore. It attains a length of two or three inches.

Lower down in sheltered places occurs our handsomest chiton, *Tonicella lineata*. The valves are usually some shade of orange or red, marked by a pattern of white and darker lines. The girdle is salmon or pinkish color and may also be banded.

The Mossy Chiton, *Mopalia muscosa,* is a dirty, light tan to greenish chiton with a thick growth of dark to almost black bristles on the girdle. This species is common on muddy bay shores, on scattered rocks and oysters, as well as on the rocky coast. It is more nearly oval in outline than most common chitons and is usually about an inch and a half long. The worn valves are greenish white; uneroded specimens have a fine pattern of beaded lines.

There are several other species of hairy-girdled chitons, two of which can be distinguished from the others by a well-defined posterior notch in the girdle. *Mopalia hindsi* has fine hairs on a light colored girdle, while *Mopalia ciliata* has denser, flatter hairs and a darker girdle. Another chiton of this group is the conspicuous Woody Chiton, *Mopalia lignosa,* with an attractive pattern of brown lines on the slate-green valves. On close examination the hairs of this species are seen to rise from light spots, and seem to be set in sockets.

Other groups of chitons have fine scales instead of bristles or hairy growths on the girdles. One of these, *Ischnochiton regularis,* is a uniform slate-green to blue.

Chitons with granular or papillose (like small fingers) ornamentation on the girdles belong to such genera as *Cyanoplax* and *Nuttallina.* There are others, but for further information, a specialist (if one can be found) should be consulted.

GASTROPODS

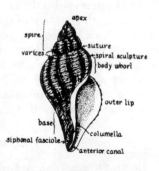

Parts of the gastropod shell

Gastropods are so named because they were thought to crawl upon their stomachs, but this is not the case. The foot is quite separate from the stomach. We characterize gastropods by the possession of an attractive, spiral shell, but many gastropods have shells without spirals, like the simple, conical limpet, or have lost them altogether, as in the large group of sea slugs or nudibranchs. Gastropods are further divided according to their internal arrangements; whether they are twisted around so the anus is at the head end (Prosobranchia), which includes most of the marine snails; whether the anus is moved toward the rear (Opisthobranchia), com-

[93]

prising the sea slugs and many small, parasitic, elaborately spired snails; or whether they have replaced their gills by lungs and have become air breathers (Pulmonata), i.e., the land snails and slugs. All three subclasses are represented in the region. However, many visitors to central California beaches, perhaps expecting drifts of handsome, brightly colored shells, are disappointed by the assemblage of small, well-camouflaged snails that occur in this region. We do have more than our share of limpets and a good representative of the most beautiful molluscs of all, the sea slugs. The latter are best observed alive; there is yet no means by which these can be preserved without losing their color and shape. To zoologists the most interesting thing about molluscs is their insides and how the rearrangements of internal anatomy serve the needs of the living animal. The shell is simply the sheltering structure secreted by the mantle, the outer layer of the animal. Persons interested only in the shells are known as conchologists; the student of the anatomy and the living animals are malacologists. Since abandoned shells are so easily collected and kept, many more kinds, especially of smaller species, will be found than we have space to consider in this small book. Unfortunately, there is no really good book about California molluscs, but all the common species can be identified with *Light's Manual*.

PROSOBRANCHIA

Our most common prosobranchs are limpets of various kinds. A limpet, according to the dictionary, is any conical herbivorous snail, and abalones are essentially large limpets as well. Limpets, however, include several rather different kinds of gastropods. In those having holes, such as the abalones and the Keyhole Limpet, *Diodora*, the gills hang in a space below the aperture, and currents of water are driven by cilia up past them and out though the holes. In this way waste material

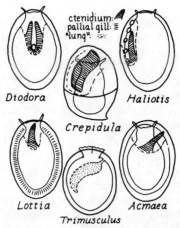

ctenidium:
pallial gill:
"lung":

Diodora   Crepidula   Haliotis

Lottia   Acmaea
Trimusculus

Arrangement of limpet respiratory systems

is prevented from settling on the gills (which we call
ctenidia in molluscs). In those limpets without holes,
but still related in structure to the holed limpets, which
include the Big Owl Limpet and our horde of Acmaeas,
the gill hangs over the top of the head and the water
current is directed from left to right across it; the anus
opens on the right side so that the waste products are
swept outside. The Owl Limpet, *Lottia,* has in addition
secondary or pallial gills developed around the margin.
Two quite different types of limpets are the Slipper and
Button Limpets. The Slipper Limpet, *Crepidula,* is not
an active grazer but lives pretty much in one place (our
common species is the black hooked shell on the surface
of turban shells) and uses its ctenidia for breathing and
food gathering, much as a clam does. The Button Limpet, *Trimusculus,* (often common in groups under overhanging rocks) has lost its gills and breathes through
the roof of its respiratory chamber; it is a pulmonate or
lunged snail related to land snails.

Most of our limpets are browsers, and when the tide
is in, they wander over the surface of the rocks, eating
diatoms and fine algae. The limpets of the higher levels,

[95]

exposed for longer periods of time, seem to be more particular about returning to a "home spot," while those of lower levels are not so dependent on a firm, well-fitted spot.

The Keyhole Limpet, *Diodora aspera*, occurs fairly low down in sheltered crevices and under stones and may be nearly two inches long. It often harbors a surprisingly large commensal polychaete, *Arctonoë vittata*, wrapped around its body at no apparent discomfort to either party concerned.

Of the several kinds of abalones occurring at various places along the California coast, two are common in the Bay region. The large red one, sought after by waders and skin divers, is *Haliotis rufescens*. The shell is somewhat wavy or irregular and often has various growths of algae, tube worms, bryozoans, etc. upon it. The Black Abalone, *Haliotis cracherodii*, is smoother and has a dark, greenish-black shell which is usually free of encrusting organisms. Specimens of the Black Abalone are occasionally seen in crevices above mid-tide level. Neither species is very common in regions accessible to hunters, although in some places, such as Tomales Point, dead shells of various sizes in good condition may be picked up on the beach. It is illegal to take abalones without a fishing license, and small ones should not be collected at any time without a scientific collecting permit, and then only if there is a serious purpose in so doing.

a: *Diodora aspera* ($\times$ 1/2); b: *Haliotus rufescens* ($\times$ 1/6);
c: *H. cracherodi* ($\times$ 1/6).

Limpets, in the strict sense, are those prosobranchs lacking holes but with ctenidia, and we have so many of them that we are not sure where to begin or end with them. Our most conspicuous limpet is the Owl Limpet, *Lottia gigantea*. This is common at Monterey and found rarely as far north as Tomales Point but not at Dillon Beach. The dark patch inside the shell is supposed to look like an owl. The common limpet of the highest tide zones north of the Bay is *Acmaea digitalis,* with its front end almost vertical or even slightly concave. The shell inside has a dark patch, which is not found in a smaller but otherwise similar limpet, *Acmaea paradigitalis.* One of the larger common limpets of intermediate levels is *Acmaea scutum,* the Plate Limpet. Perhaps the most easily identified limpet is the Dunce Cap Limpet, *Acmaea mitra,* which is a smooth white cone. It lives near the low-tide level and is often covered with a bright pink encrustation. This encrustation may be smooth or nodular; both types are a growth of coralline alga of the genus *Lithothamnion.*

A limpet of the higher rocks south of the Bay that is more common than *Acmaea digitalis* is the Rough Limpet, *Acmaea scabra,* which is flatter and has more con-

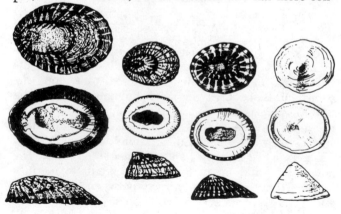

a: *Lottia gigantea;* b: *Acmaea digitalis;* c: A. *scutum;*
d: A. *mitra* (all × 2/3).

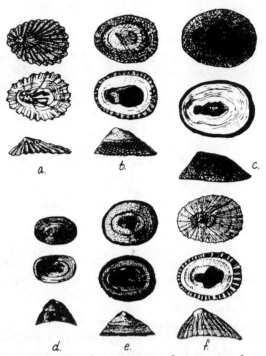

a: *Acmaea scabra;* b: *pelta;* c: *persona;* d: *insessa;* e: *fenestrata;*
f: *limatula* (all × 2/3).

spicuous ribs than *Acmaea digitalis*. Both are often
mottled or variegated like the rocks on which they live.
A dark brown, somewhat horny-textured limpet, *Acmaea insessa*, lives on seaweed, usually *Egregia;* it fits
neatly into depressions it has cut for itself along the
stipes. On Bay shores, the most common species is the
File Limpet, *Acmaea limatula;* at Monterey this species
frequents the ocean shore. There are a number of other
species, of which we offer illustrations of three: *Acmaea
pelta, Acmaea persona*, and *Acmaea fenestrata*. The
novice will find many specimens difficult to identify
because they seem to be halfway between two species,
and young specimens are, of course, hopeless. And
there are still more species.

[98]

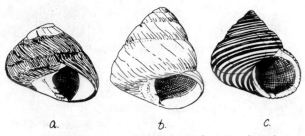

a: *Tegula funebralis* ($\times$ 1); b: *T. brunnea* ($\times$ 1);
c: *Calliostoma ligatum* ($\times$ 1½).

The Black Turban, *Tegula funebralis,* is one of the most abundant snails of the mid-tide region. About the size of a walnut, it is squat and the black surface is often eroded a dull white at the apex. The shell is particularly favored by hermit crabs as they outgrow the smaller, less capacious shells of *Thais.* The Brown Turban, *Tegula brunnea,* lives at lower levels and is taller and more massive. Only the sturdiest hermits can carry the shell about. The Top Shell, *Calliostoma ligatum,* is a smaller, more rounded and graceful shell than the turbans. The shell is brown with lighter bands and often shows blue when worn down. It is a less common species. Like the limpets, the tops and turbans are herbivores.

The littorines or periwinkles are among the characteristic small snails of the shore near high-tide level. Perhaps because of their accessibility, they have been the object of many studies. They are herbivorous snails, most often seen clustered in crevices and sheltered places. The larger one living higher up is *Littorina planaxis;* the smaller species, *Littorina scutulata,* oc-

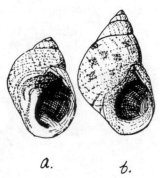

a: *Littorina planaxis;*
b: *L. scutulata* (both $\times$ 2½).

*Cerithidea
californica*
(× 1½)

curring at slightly lower levels, is somewhat taller in proportion because its shell
has more body whorls. It is difficult to tell
young and small individuals apart.

The California Horn Snail, *Cerithidea
californica,* is the most abundant snail on
mud flats, sometimes occurring in groups
of hundreds clustered around rocks and
under boards. It is a slurp feeder, living
on the film of things growing on the mud.

Our largest snail is the Moon Snail,
Polinices lewisi, whose heavy round shell
is the size of a large apple. The animal
itself is much larger when extended, and at first glance
it seems entirely too large to fit into its shell. But if
prodded enough, it forces liquid out of its mantle as it
retracts and finally closes its brown operculum neatly
behind it. Moon Snails are often seen on bay flats and
are active predators on clams. They can bore neatly

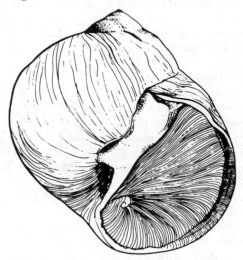

Polinices lewisi (× 1)

Olivella biplicata (× 1)

Searlesia dira (× 2/3)

tapered holes through the shells of their victims and paralyze them with toxic juices. Some people claim that Moon Snails make a fair chowder, but I have never tried it myself.

The Purple Olive, *Olivella biplicata*, is an inhabitant of clean sand near harbor mouths and may be found buried an inch or so below the surface of the sand. The shell is about one inch long, predominantly bluish lavender in color. The expanded foot of the "living shell" flares up in front of the head like a snow plow.

A rather tall, evenly tapered but dullish-colored snail, *Searlesia dira*, occurs at places like Moss Beach and Duxbury Reef but not at Dillon Beach. For some reason no one has become interested in this species, and we know almost nothing about it except that it is more abundant farther north.

The Basket Whelks and Mud Snails of the genus *Nassarius* (recognizable by the broadly open canal at the lower end of the shell) are represented by several species, including the largest of the genus, the Basket Whelk, *Nassarius fossatus*. The shell is a pretty bread-crust brown and may be nearly two inches long; the animal is an even prettier, gray speckled creature. It is common on clean tidal flats. Along the shores of San Francisco Bay is the immigrant *Nassarius obsoletus*, a dingy brown to blackish snail with a shell about half an inch long, imported, like a number of adopted Californians, from the eastern coast. The native Mud Snail, *Nassarius mendicus*, is about as unprepossessing, but the sculpturing is more pronounced and the spire of shell is taller. *Nassarius, Polinices,* and other predaceous snails that live on sandy or muddy bottoms are equipped with a natural snorkel device, the siphon. This is a tubular extension of the mantle that enables the animal to take in clean water even when burrowing about in the sediment. The Basket Whelk is an excellent species for observation of this structure in action.

A small gastropod, *Amphissa versicolor,* with shell in shades often tan, pink, or orange, which Tucker Abbott rather preciously and erroneously calls "Joseph's Coat Amphissa," may be mistaken for a *Nassarius.* It occurs on rocky shores, however, and is occasionally found as a dead shell on drifts in sheltered coves. It is really not commonly enough noticed to deserve a common name.

Two predatory snails that are especially fond of young oysters have been somewhat unnecessarily—if unintentionally—added to our fauna. Both are abundant in Tomales Bay. *Ocenebra japonica,* the Japanese Oyster Borer, is the larger, with angular whorls. From

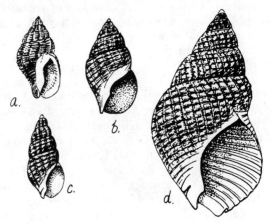

a: *Amphissa versicolor;* b: *Nassarius mendicus;* c: *N. obsoletus;* d: *N. fossatus* (all × 1½).

the Atlantic coast, brought in with Virginia oysters years ago, we have the Oyster Drill, *Urosalpinx cinereus.*

A native predator of barnacles and mussels rather than oysters is the Unicorn, *Acanthina spirata,* easily identified by its square-shouldered whorls and short spine. The Unicorn is found on ocean shores as well as along the bay, but the unwonted immigrants remain close to the oysters.

Our rock snails are poor cousins of an opulent tropical family. Some suggestion of wealthier relations can be seen in the conspicuous varices of the murex-like *Purpura foliata.* Often the shell has conspicuous, broad, brown bands. We have two species of *Thais,* related to the famous Tyrian purple snails:

Thais emarginata. This is the common predaceous snail of the upper tide levels; it feeds on barnacles and probably small mussels. The color of the shell is usually a greenish brown or grey, with darker bandings. Some young individuals are black or bright orange. The shape of the shell varies somewhat; the larger specimens with a more flaring aperture occur in the Monterey region. The eggs of this snail are contained in small yellow capsules that look like bunches of pumpkin or melon seeds.

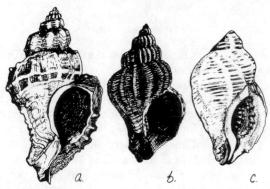

a: *Ocenebra japonica;* b: *Urosalpinx cinereus;* c: *Acanthina spirata* (all × 4/3).

[103]

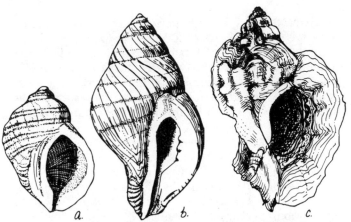

a: *Thais emarginata;* b: *Th. lamellosa;* c: *Purpura foliata* (all × 1).

Thais lamellosa. This snail is characteristic of lower tidal levels, and the shell is quite variable in shape; some are almost entirely smooth, and others show the layers which give the snail its name. Shells are usually light brown, sometimes with white bands, and occasionally light lavender or pinkish shells may be found. The variation in shell form is similar to that of the European Whelk, *Purpura lapillus.*

OPISTHOBRANCHIA

There are two major divisions of sea slugs and shell-bearing slugs. The nudibranchs have, as their name implies, naked gills or processes on the back and are often brightly colored. The gills may be in a rosette or tuft at the rear, surrounding the anus, or they may be scattered along the back. The tectibranchs have shells, often reduced to a cellophane-like piece hidden under a fold of the mantle, but in some families shells are as well developed as those of any prosobranch. However, tectibranch shells are left-handed at the beginning (and some remain so), although the young shell may be twisted around to a right-handed orientation as it grows. The gills of tectibranch slugs are carried under a flap on the right side of the animal. Most tectibranchs are herbivorous, while many nudibranchs thrive on such fare as hydroids, accumulating the unexploded nematocysts in finger-like processes along the back.

Among the dorid or dorid-like nudibranchs, the common species on rocky shores include the yellow *Anisodoris nobilis,* which characteristically has a scattering of black or dark brown tubercles over the back. This

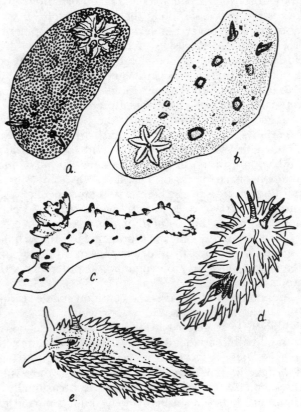

a: *Anisodoris nobilis;* b: *Diaulula sandiegensis;* c: *Triopha carpenteri;* d: *Hopkinsia rosacea;* e: *Aeolidia papillosa* (all about × 1).

may attain a size of four or five inches. A solid lemon-yellow dorid with a white rosette of gills is *Archidoris montereyensis*. Perhaps our most easily identified species is *Diaulula sandiegensis*, a pale creamy white to brownish gray species with a scattering of black oval or circular ringlike markings. This is often seen on bay flats. The triophas are among our gaudiest species and may be recognized by the rounded overhang at the front end. *Triopha carpenteri* is snow white, with clear orange processes along the back and orange splotches on the rosette. *Triopha maculata* is reddish brown, with darker red processes along the back and bluish white spots generally over the surface. The development of processes is so extensive in the cerise colored *Hopkinsia rosacea* that it is difficult to see the gill rosette; the color of this species is distinctive, however.

Among the eolids the most common species is *Hermissenda crassicornis*, whose dorsal processes (cerata) are arranged in three groups along the back. This species is variable in color, having bluish green or reddish cerata with yellow tips, but the light blue lines along the back are found in most specimens. *Hermissenda* is common on eel grass on bay flats. On some summer mornings in tide pools there may be numbers of a uniform yellowish-gray eolid with evenly arranged cerata along the back; this is *Eolidia papillosa*.

There are many other nudibranchs, but they all have one characteristic: their occurrence is unpredictable. Sometimes they may be common, at other times they are rare.

Among the tectibranchs the common species is *Phyllaplysia zostericola*, the eel grass dweller (as its name signifies). It is green like its habitat, but the body is marked with bold longitudinal stripes of black and finer cross stripes. A very large tectibranch of the genus *Aplysia*, the Sea Hare, a mottled brown, purplish, or black creature nearly a foot long, is occasionally encountered. When disturbed, it may exude a purple fluid.

The common shelled tecti-branch of our area is the Barrel Snail, *Actaeon punctocoelata,* banded black and white. It occurs on bay tidal flats.

All opisthbranchs are her-maphroditic and given to prolific reproduction; usu-ally they are to be observed producing eggs. They pro-duce eggs by the hundreds

Actaeon punctocoelata (× 3)

of thousands in egg masses shaped like spirals or pears, tear drops or strings of darning twine, and so on. The shapes of these egg masses are typical of each species.

PULMONATA

Although we have avoid-ed mention of very small species, one pulmonate about a sixteenth to an eighth of an inch long may be noticed because it is often abundant in salt marshes. This is *Ovatella myosotis,* a widespread species found in European marshes. It has gone under a variety of names. The

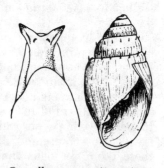

Ovatella myosotis (× 10)

specimen illustrated is a juvenile, somewhat fatter than more adult specimens, but also showing the little bris-tles around the spire that are lost in older individuals.

PELECYPODA

The pelecypods (hatchet feet), or bivalves, are less variable in shell structure than the gastropods. All our

[107]

MUSSEL   CLAM

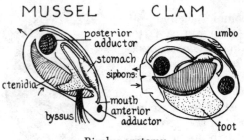

Bivalve anatomy

common species are adapted in one way or another to feeding with the gills, which are developed as elaborate accumulating structures. The food particles are moved across the gills by complex arrangements of cilia. The head is lost and the nervous system reduced to almost inconsequential ganglia, although some scallops have eyes along the edge of the mantle that are efficient detectors of shadow and movement, and thus enable the scallop to take alarm and swim clumsily away from danger.

Four orders of bivalves are recognized on the basis of gill structure. The first of these, the Protobranchia, includes the nut clams, not represented in our fauna. In these the gills are not specialized but resemble the ctenidia of limpets and topshells; the animal ploughs around in the mud to feed. Another order, the Septibranchs, live in deeper water and are not common. Two orders are represented along the shore. The first of these, the Filibranchia, have ctenidia that are not fused together to form sheets or plates, do not have siphons, and are usually attached by a byssus, a group of fibers that cements them to the substrate. The filibranchs include the mussels, scallops, and rock oysters. Scallops, the shells of Saint James as Pilgrim and of an oil company, are not found near shore in the Bay region. The order Eulamellibranchia includes most of the other bivalves. Usually these have well-developed siphons, which are tubular extensions of the mantle, and the branches of the ctenidia are folded over and joined together.

The shell of a typical clam has two more or less equal valves. Inside the valves is a line which marks the attachment of the mantle, and the space outlined by this line is the pallial sinus. When the valve is held with the inside toward the observer, the position of this line, which marks the posterior part of the shell, indicates, if it is on the right, that this is right valve, and vice versa. The outer surface of the shell is covered by the periostracum, a thin horny covering which wears off in many clams or is reduced to shreds and patches in others. At the top of the shell is the hinge, and the projection, or beak, is the umbo. The valves are held together by strong adductor muscles, whose scars are visible in most shells. The valves are pulled open by an elastic ligament across the top.

Clams and oysters are vegetarians, and require copious amounts of the enzyme amylase to digest starch. This is stored in a curious structure that is coiled about in the stomach or extended in a groove along the gut, and resembles a rod of stiff gelatin. When the clam has had a hearty meal, the rod, or crystalline style, is reduced as the enzyme is released. The style is rebuilt before the next full meal. This structure is also found in herbivorous snails and chitons. Many people fond of clams never notice this object, but are concerned that they may have a dangerous parasite when they find it for the first time. Styles would make an excellent garnish for a starchy dinner and, in fact, some Italian spaghetti dishes do include clams.

Because so many bivalves are sought after as food and thus are subject to regulations of season and bag limit, the Department of Fish and Game has tried to establish official common names for the larger species. However, other names are in common use, so we find that what we call the Washington Clam is the Butter Clam in Oregon and Washington, and what the Fish and Game people call the "Common Littleneck" is known in this area as the Rock Cockle. Regulations concerning the taking of various clams are subject to change from time to time, and the latest information is to be sought from the most up-to-date circulars of the Fish and Game Department.

FILIBRANCHIA: Mussels

The California Mussel, *Mytilus californianus,* is one of the "trade marks" of our shores. On almost every rock at mid-tide or mean sea level along the open coast, some specimens will be found. They are small and straggly away from the surf, and large and robust in massive growths or beds where wave action is heavy. The beds formed by vast numbers of mussels constitute a little universe, a habitat sheltering all sorts of animals that would otherwise be scattered in crevices and under stones at lower levels: sponges, nemerteans, worms, crabs, and snails. Mussels are excellent but dangerous eating, for their competence as filterers of fine particles makes them accumulators of the deadly *Gonyaulax* in summertime. Mussels are attached to the rocks by strong fibrous moorings, the byssus, secreted by a spe-

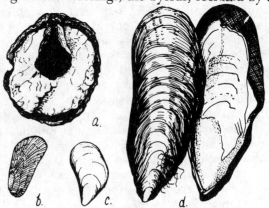

a: *Pododesmus macroschisma;* b: *Volsella demissa;* c: *Mytilus edulis;* d: *Mytilus californianus* (all about × 1/2).

cial gland. The shell of the California Mussel is heavy, with conspicuous ribbing and a brownish black covering or periostracum. Along bay shores and on piling will be found the smooth, purplish black Bay Mussel, *Mytilus edulis*. This is the common mussel of northern Europe and is also found on the Atlantic coast of America. The abundant mussel in the southern part of San Francisco Bay is the Ribbed or Horse Mussel, *Modiolus demissus*, another migrant from the eastern seaboard. The shell is brown, with prominent radiating ribs, and may grow to a length of nearly five inches. The mussel is rich in vitamins and is a potential resource for food concentrates as quick pills for executives or astronauts.

An irregular shell as large as two or three inches in diameter with a conspicuous green interior surface is often found along the ocean beach. This is the upper valve of the Rock Oyster, or Jingle, *Pododesmus macroschisma*, The lower valve is thin and fits closely to the rock or abalone to which the animal is attached by a byssus through a hole near the hinge. The Rock Oyster has bright orange flesh and is the finest flavored bivalve in our fauna. From Pigeon Point southward, a smaller Jingle, *Anomia peruviana*, with a salmon or amber translucent shell is occasionally found in places where shells accumulate.

LAMELLIBRANCHIA: Oysters and clams

Oysters, esteemed since Roman times, are creatures of bays and other sheltered waters. Our native oyster, *Ostrea lurida*, is small and, while of fine flavor, is not raised commercially in this region. It is common in Tomales Bay, settling on rocks, piling, and the shells of the Japanese Oyster (now politically renamed Pacific Oyster), *Crassostrea gigas*. The Japanese Oyster does not grow naturally in the Bay region but is brought over as spat—young, just settled oysters—from Japan and raised in Drakes Estero and Tomales Bay, where it

Ostrea lurida (× 1/2)   *Crassostrea gigas* (× 1/3)

grows very rapidly, attaining a size of several inches in two years. This is the large chalky oyster with an undistinguished flavor. Some Eastern Oysters, *Crassostrea virginica*, are also to be found in Tomales Bay. These oysters are smaller, with much heavier shells and a dark muscle scar. The Olympia Oyster can be told from both of these by the small teeth which can be felt by the fingernail at the base of the hinge. Oysters were once a thriving industry in San Francisco Bay. The loss of this picturesque and valuable enterprise is one of the many prices we have had to pay for progress.

One of the characteristic features of sandy flats is the scattering of thin white shells of sand clams. In life the clams live several inches to more than a foot beneath the surface, and their presence is revealed only by digging. The larger Sand Clam, *Macoma secta*, favors the higher sand flats near bay mouths. Both valves are flat and plate-like and specimens may attain a length of about three inches. The smaller Bent-nosed Clam, *Macoma nasuta*, has both valves bent slightly at the posterior end and frequents bottoms where mud is mixed with sand. While both species are of good flavor, it is difficult to clean the sand out, so they are not often sought as food. The Macomas are "vacuum cleaner"

Macoma secta ($\times$ 2/3)　　　　　*Macoma nasuta* ($\times$ 2/3)

clams, with two long siphons, one inhalant, the other exhalant. The inhalant siphon sweeps over the surface, sucking in nutritious detritus from the bottom. The detached siphons may writhe about for some time and have led many students astray.

The Jackknife Clam, *Tagelus californianus*, has separate siphons like the sand clams, but they are short and stubby. It has a grayish-white shell about four inches long and is more common in the southern part of our area, from Elkhorn Slough southwards, although it occurs in bays as far north as Humboldt. The hinge of the Jackknife Clam is near the middle, while that of Razor Clams is off center. Our Razor Clam, *Siliqua patula*, is a much larger clam, reaching six or seven inches in length, and has a smooth, heavy yellow-brown periostracum. Inside the shell there is a conspicuous ridge from the umbo to the margin of the shell. Razor clams live on open sandy beaches and are highly esteemed as food.

Tagelus californianus ($\times$ 1/2)　　　　*Siliqua patula* ($\times$ 1/2)

Our two largest clams are not closely related except in superficial appearance and habitat. Both have very long, heavy, single siphons which make up most of the bulk of the animal, and the two clams may be instantly told apart by the tips of the siphons. In the Gaper or Horse Clam, *Tresus* (long known as *Schizothaerus*) *nuttalli*, there are leathery or horny flaps on either side of the tip, whereas the Goeduck, *Panope generosa*, is unadorned. The Gaper is a representative of the Mactridae; the Goeduck belongs to the Saxicavidae. The shell of the Gaper is more oval in outline and deeply dished, making it a convenient ash tray, while that of the Goeduck is shallower and rectangular at the siphon (posterior) end. Gapers are among our most abundant clams, occurring on all bay shores and in sandy places among rocks on sheltered ocean beaches. Their oval holes, often with the siphons protruding, are conspicuous; when disturbed by a pedestrian, or when the tide is coming in, the siphon is retracted with a resulting squirt of water. Gapers are found along the entire California coast and north to Alaska; toward the north there are specimens with more rounded, deeper shells which are probably *Tresus* (=*Schizothaerus*) *capex*. The Goeduck is more abundant in Puget Sound, but there are always a few mingled with Gapers in California clam-

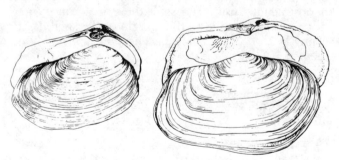

Tresus nuttalli (× 1/5)   *Panope generosa* (× 1/5)

[114]

ming beds. It is even larger than the Gaper: specimens weighing up to forty founds have been taken in Puget Sound according to chamber of commerce brochures, but eight to twelve pounds is the maximum an ordinary mortal can expect. Both clams live in vertical burrows several feet deep, and capturing them requires some skill beyond the brute force of digging a large hole in the mud and smashing all manner of innocent invertebrates that happen to be in the way. One of the popular methods is to use a length of drain pipe as a caisson, and there are some skillful and devoted clammers willing to lie prone in the mud who can take them by hand.

Cockles are round, short-siphoned clams with comparatively heavy shells. The true cockles of the family *Cardiidae* have a heart-shaped outline when viewed from the end. The Basket, or Heart Cockle, *Clinocardium nuttalli*, is an inhabitant of sandy areas near bay mouths, where it lives close to the surface. Sometimes live specimens are found on the surface at low tide. The Rock Cockles (of the family Veneridae) do not have the prominent interlocking ribs along the margin like the Basket Cockle; the former are usually found in sandy mud among rocks, or under large loose rocks. Our common native species is the Rock Cockle, *Protothaca staminea*, but it seems to be giving way to the more

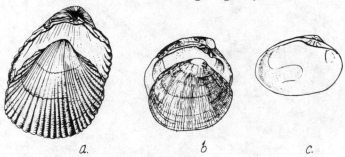

a.   b.   c.

a: *Clinocardium nuttalli;* b: *Protothaca staminea;* c: *Tapes semidecussata* (all × 1/2).

ovate, lighter-shelled Japanese Cockle, *Tapes semide-cussata*, which was apparently introduced about 1930 and is now common from Elkhorn Slough to British Columbia. All three species are prettily marked with zig-zagged, light brown bands and stripes when young; often these colors disappear with age, and older shells are a uniform light brown in the Basket Cockle and grayish-white in the Rock Cockle.

A large venerid often found by diggers in pursuit of Gapers is the Washington Clam, *Saxidomus nuttalli*, distinctive for its heavy shell with a purple tinge at the posterior end and the strong concentric ridges on the exterior. California's most famous venerid is the Pismo Clam, *Tivela stultorum*, which is abundant on the open sandy beaches of some parts of southern California. The Pismo Clam has a dense, heavy shell, roughly triangular in outline, that may be as long as seven inches. The shell is covered by a shiny brown periostracum that looks like a coat of varnish. Young specimens have contrasting rays of darker brown to purplish. The flesh is pink with hemoglobin. The northern limit of the Pismo Clam is the beach between Watsonville and Monterey.

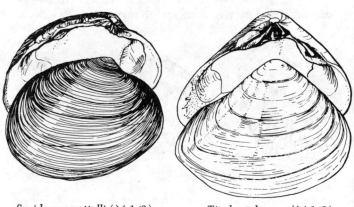

Saxidomus nuttalli (× 1/3)   *Tivela stultorum* (× 1/3)

Mya arenaria (× 1/2)

On bay shores, often in mud that is unpleasantly dirty, a dingy gray, fragile-shelled clam with a thick, stubby siphon is sometimes common. This is the Eastern Soft Shell Clam, *Mya arenaria*, one of our earliest marine immigrants to make the trip with oysters from the Atlantic coast. It arrived sometime in the 1870's and is now found from Elkhorn Slough to British Columbia.

There are many species of boring clams inhabiting soft rocks and thick mud. They are most common in such areas as Duxbury Reef, Moss Beach, and other places where they can bore into the rock; they are rare at Monterey and north of Duxbury because the rocks are too hard. The Peapod Borer, *Botula falcata*, is related to the mussels. It has a rich brown periostracum and is perhaps not a real borer at all, but a nestler in holes made by the true borers. These latter are members of the Pholadidae, related to the infamous shipworms (*Teredo*). There are several species of pholads in our area. One of the common species is *Pholadidea penita*. Our largest species is the Rough Piddock, *Zirfaea pilsbryi*, a denizen of heavy mud in bays. The piddocks bore by attaching their strong foot and rotating the roughened part of the shell, rasping a hole slowly as they grow. The shipworms, which retain only this rasping part of the shell at the end of a long worm-like body, are able to bore into wood.

Botula falcata (× 1)

Pholadidea penita (× 1)

[117]

The cephalopods, or head-feet, include the Octopoda, or octopuses, with eight arms and sessile suckers; the Decapoda, or squids, with ten arms and stalked suckers; and *Nautilus*, a relic of a once numerous company that went into a decline in Mesozoic times. Another group, the Ammonoids, has left no survivors in our times; their fossils may be found in Cretaceous rocks.

Squids are rapidly swimming, predaceous animals. One species, *Loligo opalescens*, is often abundant in Monterey Bay, where it is fished for bait and food. This squid apparently comes near shore to breed, and divers may observe its egg masses, which are white cylindrical objects attached by a stalk to the bottom. Specimens can often be obtained from bait stands and larger fish markets in the Bay region.

Octopuses are not common in our latitudes in shore pools, but small specimens are occasionally observed at very low summer tides. These are probably *Octopus appolyon*. Octopuses are mildly venomous and are known to cause painful wounds. They are delicate animals to keep in captivity as they need lots of clean, cold water. Even in the big public aquaria, where they receive the best of care, they do not live long.

Octopus sp. (× 1)

BRYOZOA and ENTOPROCTA: Moss animals

The two phyla included here are actually not related except in superficial appearance, but they are usually included together for convenience in systematic monographs. The entoprocts, or nodding heads, do not have a coelom but do have a pair of protonephridia, and the anus opens within the circle of tentacles. Our common species is *Barentsia gracilis,* abundant in some parts of San Francisco Bay in spring, appearing as felt-like aggregations on piling and floats. It is only two or three millimeters high.

The bryozoans have a coelom and lack nephridia; there are numerous species on this coast. Bryozoans are characteristically colonial organisms, forming crusts or leaf-like colonies on the surface of rocks, old shells, or algae, or forming solitary bushy or gelatinous colonies. Some of these may be several inches high. The individual bryozoan, or polypide, occupies a case termed the zooecium (animal house). The body can be retracted, apparently instantaneouly, into this house by special muscles, and in many species there is a little cover, or

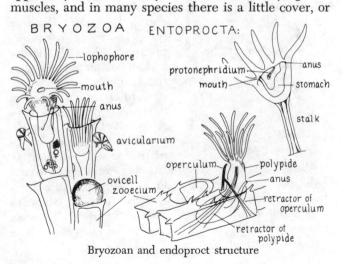

Bryozoan and endoproct structure

operculum, that closes over it. The tentacles form a horseshoe-shaped structure, the lophophore, surrounding the mouth; the anus opens separately.

In many colonies some individual polypides are modified to form curious structures resembling birds' beaks, termed avicularia. These apparently keep the colony free of foreign objects by picking them off. In some Bryozoa the young are developed in special ovicells; in others the zooecium is not modified. Identification of the species requires close microscopic examination of many fine structures; use of the synopsis should at least help the reader decide whether his specimen is a bryozoan or not.

PHORONIDA

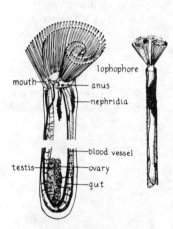

Phoronid structure:
Phoronopsis harmeri ($\times$ 1).

Phoronida constitute a small phylum of two genera and a dozen species of worm-like creatures with a prominent lophophore of a double crescent of tentacles and a U-shaped digestive tract. There is a pair of nephridia and a circulatory system containing hemoglobin. Our species, *Phoronopsis harmeri*, is very common indeed, occurring in extensive beds at half-tide levels, where its pale green lophophores are conspicuous in shallow standing water or its numerous small round holes perforate the bare sand. The tube is a stiff structure embedded with sand grains; large populations of these phoronids hold the sand flat together. The sexes are separate. Phoronids have peculiar elaborate larvae called actinotrochs.

BRACHIOPODA

The brachiopods, or lamp shells, are rare in our area, since they live mostly in deep water. They share with phoronids and bryozoans the crown of tentacles or lophophore, but they possess bivalved shells resembling those of clams, though oriented from top to bottom instead of left and right; they are attached by a peduncle which enters the lower valve. *Terebratalia transversa*, with a reddish shell, is rarely found at very low tide.

Another species, *Glottidia alba*, occurs rarely in bay bottoms. It does not look very different from *Lingula*, a brachiopod genus that has been in existence since Paleozoic times. In those distant days brachiopods were once among the most numerous animals of the sea; the living brachiopods are impoverished descendants of a once glorious and aristocratic line.

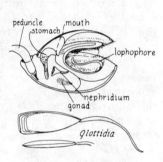

Brachiopod structure and *Glottidia alba* ($\times$ 1/2)

ECHINODERMA
(Plate 8)

The creatures known as echinoderms are among the most curious of all animals, so different in some ways that they might have come from another planet. They are exclusively creatures of the sea, and their best-known representative type, the starfish, or sea star, is as characteristic of the seashore as the sand itself. The phylum Echinoderma, or Echinodermata, is characterized by a symmetry of five radiating divisions; a calcareous skeleton, often with spines, covered by an almost invisible skin; and a strange internal hydraulic or "water vascular" system. This system consists of a sort of filter plate, the "sieve plate" or "madreporite," through which water is drawn into the stone canal by ciliary action; a central ring with radiating vessels along the arms; and in most starfish and sea urchins at least, a double row of "tube feet"—little structures with suction cups at their outer ends and a bulb-like muscular pumping structure internally. With these tube feet the animal can move and, to some extent, breathe; using them, the sea star is capable of hanging on with such force that it is possible for a starfish with the aid of hundreds of its tube feet to pull a mussel open wide enough to slip its bag-like eversible stomach into the narrow gap. At the same time it releases a poison that relaxes its victim. One of the most amazing things about the echinoderms is that in development of intestinal cavities and their type of bilateral, free-swimming larvae, they most resemble some primitive relatives of the vertebrates. If not closely related to men and fishes, they at least have some startling resemblances that suggest kindred lines of descent. Despite these suggestions of relationship, echinoderms have a rather crude nervous system, without any brain or coördinating center. In the earlier days of zoology the echinoderms were grouped with the jellyfish and hydroids as the Radiata, because they possess in common an apparently radial symmetry.

The four classes of echinoderms represented in our fauna are illustrated in Plate 8. These are the Asteroidea, the sea stars; the Ophiuroidea, the brittle or serpent stars; the Echinoidea, urchins and sand dollars; and the Holothuroidea, the sea cucumbers. A fifth class, Crinoidea, sea lilies or feather stars, is not found in this area and most of its members are deep water creatures. In Paleozoic seas they were among the most abundant of animals of which we have record. A feather star, *Antedon*, is found in Puget Sound.

There is something appealing about natural geometry, and it is a universal impulse, on first encountering a sea star, to take it home. The end result, even with the best of care, including a preliminary bath in formaldehyde and drying in the sun, is sad; the creature collapses and shrivels, the colors quickly fade, and finally the once beautiful specimens resemble nothing so much as pieces of weather-bleached carton. Too often, however, the specimens are forgotten in the family car and hastily disposed of a few days later.

ASTEROIDEA: Sea Stars
(Plate 4)

The most common sea star of our coast, from Canada to Baja California, is the Ochre Star, *Pisaster ochraceous*. This sea star occurs in several colors: an orange or yellow ochre, brown, purple, and some intermediate shades. It is invariably one or another of these colors, not mottled. It lives near mid-tide level, and when the tide is out it is often found near the bottom of rocks or in crevices, although some specimens may be found still embracing the mussels upon which they feed. A related star, *Pisaster brevispinus*, is invariably pink and has shorter spines; it is characteristic of softer bottoms and lower levels.

In the larger tide pools a huge sea star, with 21 rays or "arms" (more or less), is often encountered. This is the Sunflower Star, *Pycnopodia helianthoides*. It is capable of rather active movement for a starfish and can sometimes be seen gliding across the sandy bottom of a large pool. It is usually of an orange reddish color. The pedicellariae are very large, and their action may be felt by laying the back of the hand on the surface so that the pedicellariae catch the hairs.

The Bat Star or Webbed Star, *Patiria miniata*, is sometimes almost as common as the Ochre Star. It is easily identified by its short arms and broadened disc which give it an appearance of being webbed between the arms. Its most frequent color in the region seems to be

[123]

orange, sometimes as bright as a piece of orange peel, but specimens of two colors, like irregular mosaic, are common. A beginner might mistake the Bat Star for another star with somewhat longer arms, but smooth and moist to the touch; this is *Dermasterias imbricata*, the Leather Star.

There are several small sea stars which are often common. The comparatively slender, gracefully proportioned rays distinguish these smaller species from young pisasters. The most conspicuous of these is the bright red *Henricia leviuscula*. A smaller, greenish, six-rayed star is *Leptasterias aequalis*.

Ophiuroidea: Brittle Stars

At very low tides, under stones and among the surf-grass roots and kelp holdfasts, brittle stars or serpent stars may be found.

Several kinds look about the same and require painstaking study of spines and plates about the mouth to identify. One species is easily distinguished because of the small scales on its upper (aboral) surface, and its short stout arms with very short spines. This is *Ophio-*

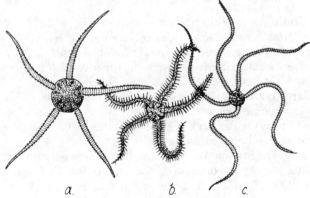

a: *Ophioplocus esmarki;* b: *Ophiothrix spiculata;* c: *Amphiodia occidentalis* (all × 1).

[124]

plocus esmarki; its color is dull brown. The fragile brittle star with the long spines and orange bands on the arms is probably *Ophiothrix spiculata*. Serpent stars with very long arms, eight or ten times as long as the diameter of the disc, are members of the genus *Amphiodia*. These stars live buried in sand on bay shores where the water is clean. There are at least ten, perhaps more than a dozen, common brittle stars in our area.

ECHINOIDEA: Sea Urchins, Sand Dollars

Two species of sea urchins are common in our region; both of them frequent outer reefs where surf is heavy. They are common therefore on the outer coasts. The smaller, Purple Urchin, *Strongylocentrotus purpuratus*, is more common and sometimes very abundant. It occupies circular pits where the rock is soft enough. The larger urchin, *Strongylocentrotus franciscanus*, is a dark red, with proportionately larger spines; it occurs in somewhat deeper water or farther out from shore than the Purple Urchin.

Sand Dollar

We have only one species of sand dollar in this region, *Dendraster excentricus*. It occurs in beds in sandy bottoms, and the specimens usually found on the beach are the dead tests. In life this white "shell" is covered with a furry coat of short, greenish gray spines.

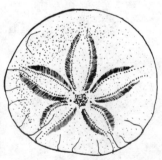

Dendraster excentricus (× 1/2)

HOLOTHUROIDEA: Sea Cucumbers

Holothurians are not too abundant, but two species

Cucumaria miniata (× 1/2)

are often encountered. On vertical and overhanging surfaces of large rocks there may be seen dense aggregations of slug-like, black cucumbers perhaps an inch long; these may also be seen among the mussels. This is *Cucumaria curata*. The large *Cucumaria miniata*, with dark orange body and bright orange tentacles, is sometimes abundant in crevices near low tide level.

CHAETOGNATHA: Arrow Worms

The chaetognaths, or arrow worms, are a phylum of perhaps 50 or 60 species of predaceous planktonic organisms. They are restricted to the open seas, and only rarely can one be caught near shore. The distribution of these creatures sometimes provides clues about the origin of waters or the direction of currents in the oceans. Hence, they are significant beyond their numbers, as far as oceanographers are concerned, although they are abundant enough at times. To the zoologists they constitute a puzzle. They appear to have

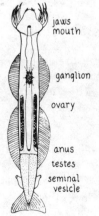

Chaetognath structure

the primitive division of the coelom into three parts which is characteristic of chordates, but they are unique in having the reproductive cells differentiated well before any recognizable differentiation of other organs begins. They are always hermaphroditic, although both sexes may not be mature at the same time, but very little is known of their sexual economy. So far it has been impossible to raise them in captivity. Some species are less than an inch long; others may attain lengths of three inches or more. The best known genus is *Sagitta*.

CHORDATA: Tunicates

The chordates are so named because they possess, at one stage or another, a reinforcing structure along the back, the notochord. In the vertebrates, that group of chordates in which we include ourselves, the backbone is developed around this chord. Other characteristics of the chordates are the possession of gill slits—passages through the region back of the mouth to the exterior— and the location of the nerve chord along the back, above the notochord. The most primitive chordates are the tunicates, whose chordate affinities are obvious only in the larval stage. This larva looks somewhat like a tadpole, with a strong muscular tail reinforced by a notochord. In other respects the tadpole is not too different from the adult tunicate, and metamorphosis of the latter consists principally in losing the tail and notochord and reorienting the front part to suit the sedentary or floating life of the adult tunicate.

Essentially, a tunicate, or Sea Squirt, is a series of bags within bags. Outermost, there is the tunic, made partly of a substance resembling cellulose, the stuff of which trees are made, in which is a sac, the mantle, surrounding an internal cavity, the atrium. The atrium has two apertures, and inside it is the body proper of the animal. One aperture, the mouth, leads into a pharynx, with numerous slits or holes, the stigmata, allowing the

[127]

passage of water out into the atrium and thence outside via the excurrent aperture of the atrium. Along the ventral surface of the pharynx is the endostyle, a groove which secretes mucus that aids in trapping food. The pharynx is also the principal respiratory organ. To this day, as anyone who swallows a bit carelessly knows,

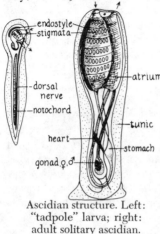

feeding and breathing have been intimately associated. Indeed, chordates are not unique in this dual purpose; molluscs have carried it to a fine art. The tunicates, however, are filtering animals par excellence, and many of them are expert chemists. Some tunicates can accumulate vanadium (so rare in sea water that most methods of chemical analysis cannot detect it) to concentrations some 250,000 times that found in sea water.

Ascidian structure. Left: "tadpole" larva; right: adult solitary ascidian.

Tunicates are hermaphroditic in their sexually mature stage, but many species reproduce by budding or sexless dividing to form chains, rosettes, or massive, lump-like colonies.

Properly speaking, the Sea Squirts, those sessile double-spouted bags, should be referred to as ascidians, since the tunicates include the pelagic salps (chains of individuals) and appendicularians—tadpole larvae that have grown up to adulthood without losing their tails. There are several types of ascidians. The solitary ascidians are the Sea Squirts such as *Ascidia ceratodes* (and *Ciona*, introduced in our synopsis) and the leathery *Styela montereyensis*. These are often found along rocky shores. *Ciona* is conspicuous on piling, along with a dingy gray thing about the size of a marble that is a native of the east coast, as its name suggests: *Mol-*

gula manhattensis. Then there are the social ascidians, which live in clusters joined together by stolons like strawberry plants, or with individuals coalescing at the base, like *Clavelina huntsmani.* The compound ascidians are often large aggregations of minute individuals in a fleshy, common matrix. Among these are the Sea Pork, *Amaroucium,* and other genera.

a: *Ascidia ceratodes;*
b: *Clavelina huntsmani;*
c: *Styela montereyensis;*
d: *Molgula manhattensis*
   (all × 1/2).

More than twenty species of social and compound ascidians have been recognized from local shores, and there are about as many solitary species. Some of them look like small grapes, or little red balls, and others are shaped (but not colored) like the sack of a bagpipe.

MAMMALIA

Although the mammals have gone to considerable evolutionary effort to become terrestrial, air-breathing creatures, a number of them have re-invaded the sea. Three orders of mammals are represented in the sea: Carnivora, Pinnipedia, and Cetacea. A few representatives of a fourth, Primates, are currently engaged in a limited invasion of shallow waters with diving apparatus and of the deepest ocean in small steel balls.

The carnivores are represented by the Sea Otter, *Enhydra lutris,* a marine member of the otter and weasel family. The Sea Otter was once very abundant along our shores and was the major economic motivation for much of the early exploration and exploitation of the California coast. Now the southern race is restricted to a population of about 600 in small herds, from Point

Lobos to the Santa Barbara Islands. Sea otters are rather shy and frequent the kelp beds, where their heads are not easily distinguished from the large kelp bladders. They feed on sea urchins, abalones, crabs, and other succulent invertebrates which they bring to the surface and open by smashing the catch against a rock held on the breast. The fur of the Sea Otter is the finest of all furs in a group notable for its excellent fur, and the Sea Otter is rigidly protected. Sea Otters are more abundant in the Aleutians than along California at this time. There are frequently rumors that they have been sighted at Año Nuevo Island and off the Sonoma coast. So far there has been no verification, and those who wish to be sure of seeing Sea Otters must travel south of Monterey with a pair of strong field glasses.

The Sea Otter is 3 to 5 feet long, floats on its back among the kelp beds. The older males have whitish heads. The females mature in about four years and bear one pup at a time, born at sea.

Several species of pinnipedes are abundant in our coastal waters, as testified by the name Seal Rocks, off San Francisco, for one of their favorite assembly grounds. The name "seal" is loosely applied to two different groups of pinnipedes, the eared seals and sea lions, and the true seal, which lacks external ears. The large conspicuous mammals seen on the rocks are bull sea lions.

The Steller Sea Lion, *Eumetopias jubata,* is lighter in color (the fur is brown when dry) than the darker, nearly black California Sea Lions, *Zalophus californianus.*

The cows are not easy to tell apart from a distance, but the bulls are distinctive. The much larger Steller has a light-colored mane and a low-browed forehead, while the California Sea Lion has a crest, giving it a high-browed appearance, and is a uniform, dark, seal brown. The big Steller bulls may weigh up to a ton; the California bulls attain about half the size and weight of the Stellers. The two species occur together along this coast except during the summer months, when the Californias are absent. The Stellers breed from the Channel Islands north to Alaska. The pups are born on the rocky haul-out grounds in June and July, and breeding follows immediately. The California Sea Lions breed from the Channel Islands south. Usually only one pup is born at a time to females of either species, and is able to swim a few minutes after birth. Populations of both species occur at Año Nuevo Island, although only the Steller Sea Lion breeds there. They also occur on the Farallons and at Point Reyes. The California Sea Lion is the familiar trained seal of circus and zoological garden. There is a regular academy for training seals at the San Diego Zoo, and the graduates are exchanged with other zoos for other exhibits.

There is a perennial argument between naturalists and fishermen about the damage sea lions may do to fish, especially salmon. Since the first California Fish and Game Commission met, about 1874, there have been demands for the extermination of the sea lions to improve the fishing. Naturalists believe the levies taken by sea lions of desirable fish are comparatively insignificant; they point out that, as far as salmon are concerned, the best way to restore the great salmon populations of the past would be to knock out the dams on spawning streams and limit the population of people. Año Nuevo Island, which has always had heavy concentrations of sea lions, is well known to sport fishermen as an excellent place for bottom fishing.

The most common true seal of our waters is the Harbor Seal, *Phoca vitulina*. This is a small, spotted seal, often occupying the same rocks with the sea lions, but also common on sand bars near harbor mouths. A sizeable herd of Harbor Seals may often be seen by Bay Bridge commuters on a large sand bar exposed at low tide to the north of the east on-ramp of the bridge. The Harbor Seal is about five feet long. One pup is born, in

Local marine mammals. In the far background, the Killer Whale, *Orcinus orca* (behind the Gray Whale, *Eschrichtius glaucus*). Upper left, the Steller Sea Lion, *Eumetopias jubata*, cow and bull; two young bull Elephant Seals, *Mirounga angustirostris,* immediately below. Center left, a Sea Otter, *Enhydra lutris;* center right, a bull California Sea Lion, *Zalophus californianus.* Immediately below, a Harbor Seal, *Phoca vitulina.* Bottom: *Homo sapiens scaphandris.*

early spring. Occasionally a pup strays from its mother in the surf at such places as Dillon Beach and some kind person "rescues" it. It is best to let nature—and mother —take care of such strays.

The Harbor Seal has a very wide range, occurring along the shores of northwestern Europe to the Bay of Biscay, the Atlantic coast of America to about Cape Hatteras, and in the Pacific Ocean from the Chukchi Sea southward to Mexico in the east and to the Yellow Sea in the west. It has been found in Hudson Bay and Lake Ontario. The Pacific coast race is named *Phoca vitulina richardi.*

Our largest seal is the Northern Elephant Seal, *Mirounga angustirostris.* The bulls of this species attain a weight of about two and a half tons; they develop a large proboscis which is inflated as a warning device, and with which they produce a racket that sounds like a heavy truck going uphill. The elephant seal was once thought to be extinct, but there are perhaps 15,000 of them now, frequenting the outer Channel Islands and Guadalupe Island off Baja California. There is a small population at Año Nuevo Island. The Elephant Seal can be distinguished by its light brown color, and also by its reluctance to move off the beach, sometimes until prodded into movement. Its movement on land is like that of a large maggot, but it is, like all seals, a power-ful, graceful swimmer. It feeds on sharks, rays, and squid, and may descend several hundred feet.

Whales and porpoises are the most marine of all the sea-going mammals, and are unable to survive when stranded. Along the shore, two whales are occasionally seen. The California Gray Whale, *Eschrichtius glaucus,* is a coastal species, migrating from Arctic waters in win-ter to calve and breed in the lagoons of Baja California. Occasionally a Gray Whale is seen in San Francisco or Tomales Bay. Other than being a whale, it is not much to look at. It has no dorsal fin and the straight back has a series of bumps toward the posterior end near the flukes, and it is usually so covered with barnacles that it has an old, waterlogged appearance. The spout is low, directed slightly forward, and diffuse, like a poorly functioning garden spray. Gray Whales return from Baja California in spring, and stragglers may be seen in this area in summer. Once almost exterminated, the Gray Whale is slowly increasing under rigid international protection. The Gray Whale attains a length of from thirty to fifty feet and a weight of perhaps twenty tons.

The Killer Whale, or Orca, *Orcinus orca*, may be seen from time to time, sometimes in groups (pods). It can be identified, as far as it can be seen, by its high straight dorsal fin and the conspicuous white markings on the black body; it may grow as large as thirty feet in length. As their name implies, Killer Whales are ferocious predators and will attack whales, porpoises, and seals.

The Killer Whale is actually a large porpoise. In these days of bridges and high-speed traffic there is little opportunity, except for those who have their own boats, to observe porpoises in San Francisco Bay. Two species are recorded from the Bay. The Dall Porpoise, *Phocoenoides dalli* (five to six feet long), is prettily marked with black and white and has small flippers. The Bay Porpoise, *Phocaena vomerina*, is somewhat larger, dark above and light below (but not the dazzling white of the Dall Porpoise), and with a blunter snout.

At the present time a whaling station is operated in San Francisco Bay at Point San Pablo, Richmond. Humpback, Sei, Fin-back, and Sperm whales are caught at sea and brought in for processing, mostly to be canned as pet food. (Thus have we fallen from the days of Capts. Ahab and Scammon!) These whales are only rarely seen from shore, although a dead one occasionally drifts ashore, causing local disposal problems.

The most recent addition to our marine mammal fauna is *Homo sapiens*, equipped with various prosthetic devices to aid in respiration and to protect him from low water temperatures. Usually these are males, bent on piscicide or abalone gathering, but females are becoming more common. These new invaders of the sea are best observed on weekends in fair weather. A somewhat rare subspecies, which we hope will become more common, is interested in studying marine life under water in a more scientific spirit. A regrettable tendency of some of the more gregarious divers is the mass destruction of starfish; this group activity is motivated by the unverified assumption that all starfish are bad and that their removal will improve all manner of things which seem to be of more importance to man. If we were to extend this idea to everything that "competes with" or eats something we want to eat, a surprising number of the familiar seashore animals would have to be exterminated.

SOME REFERENCES

The books listed below provide more detail about our shore life than is possible in this book, or they supply general background information. The *Light Manual* and Ricketts and Calvin both have excellent bibliographies, and from them one who wishes to go further can find his way. Therefore, no attempt has been made to list such things as seashell guides, crustacean monographs, and the like.

Buchsbaum, Ralph. *Animals Without Backbones: An Introduction to the Invertebrates.* University of Chicago Press, 1948.
 A very good introduction.
Defant, Albert. *Ebb and Flow: The Tides of Earth, Air, and Water.* Ann Arbor: University of Michigan Press, 1958.
 Available as a paperback.
Emery, K. O. *The Sea Off Southern California: A Mod-*

ern Habitat of Petroleum. New York: John Wiley and Sons, 1961.

Comprehensive account of oceanographic work done off southern California.

Light, S. F., rev. by Smith, R. I., Pitelka, Frank A., Abbott, Donald P., and Weesner, Frances M., with many others. *Intertidal Invertebrates of the Central California Coast.* Berkeley and Los Angeles: University of California Press, 1954.

In some groups excellent, in others frustrating—a reflection on the animals, not the contributors.

Norris, Kenneth S. and Prescott, John H. *Observations on Pacific Cetaceans of Californian and Mexican Waters.* University of California Publications in Zoölogy, Vol. 63, No. 4, pp. 291–402, pls. 27–41, 1961.

Mostly about porpoises.

Ricketts, Edward F., and Calvin, Jack. (Revised by Joel W. Hedgpeth) *Between Pacific Tides.* Third edition, revised. Stanford: Stanford University Press, 1962.

This edition includes a chapter on marine ecology and a revised bibliography.

Russell, R. C. H., and Macmillan, D. H. *Waves and Tides.* New York: Philosophical Library, 1953.

Scheffer, Victor B. *Seals, Sea Lions, and Walruses: A Review of the Pinnipeda.* Stanford: Stanford University Press, 1958.

Contains most of the information known about the distribution, breeding, etc., of these animals.

Smith, Gilbert M. *Marine Algae of the Monterey Peninsula, California.* Stanford: Stanford University Press, 1944.

Essential for the seaweeds.

Walford, Lionel A. *Living Resources of the Sea: Opportunities for Research and Expansion.* New York: The Ronald Press, 1958.

The best available treatment of this subject.